I Choose To Be A *Lady*

Basic Life Lessons for Our Daughters

I Choose To Be A Lady

Basic Life Lessons for Our Daughters

Kiana Shaw

I CHOOSE TO BE A LADY
Published by Purposely Created Publishing Group™

Copyright © 2016 Kiana Shaw

ALL RIGHTS RESERVED.

No part of this book may be reproduced, distributed or transmitted in any form by any means, graphics, electronics, or mechanical, including photocopy, recording, taping, or by any information storage or retrieval system, without permission in writing from the publisher, except in the case of reprints in the context of reviews, quotes, or references.

Printed in the United States of America

ISBN (paperback): 978-1-945558-05-4

ISBN (ebook): 978-1-945558-06-1

Special discounts are available on bulk quantity purchases by book clubs, associations and special interest groups. For details email:
sales@publishyourgift.com
or call (888) 949-6228.

For information log on to:
www.PublishYourGift.com

This book is dedicated to:

My amazing daughter, Kayla Renee. Mommy is in awe of you and I love you with every molecule that makes up my being. You are my reason to succeed, not my excuse to fail. There is nothing I won't do for you. You amaze me every single day with your charm, your brilliance and your capacity to love me unconditionally. Someday, you will be able to read this book for yourself and I pray it is simply a reiteration of what I have already taken the time to teach you. However, if for some reason that I am not here to tell you, please take this book as a guide of what I want you to know. I love you, Tuga! #KaylaMomma

My lovely nieces: Jasmine, Taylor, Kaylee, Ky'Aira, and Regan. You ladies are amazingly beautiful with great hearts and minds. I have been blessed beyond measure to be your auntie and have you all in my world. You inspire me to be the best me possible, and this book is in dedication of you—you all were my daughters first. Thank you for loving me and I pray that you are proud of this book. #AuntiesBabies

And for the teen girls who have gone through Village of Truth, Inc. and LeadHERship Academy, LLC: I have spent almost ten years giving you all the best of me. I pray this book reaffirms and reminds you of all of the lessons I have taught you.

Table of Contents

Dedication ... v

Acknowledgements ... ix

Special Thank You ... xi

Foreword ... xii

Preface ... xv

What Is a Lady: Why Would I Want to Be One? ... 1

Feminine Hygiene: Ladies Leave Behind a Scent, Not an Odor ... 5

Controlling Your Weight: Ladies Know They Are More Than a Number on a Scale ... 25

Sex: Ladies Make Informed Decisions About Sex ... 35

Self-Esteem: Ladies Love Themselves First ... 47

Social Media: Ladies Use the Internet Responsibly ... 61

Professional Development: Ladies Are Prepared for What They Want ... 71

Goal Setting: Ladies Make Plans ... 81

Bullying: Ladies Don't Intentionally Hurt People ... 89

Dating: Ladies Know They Can't Turn a Cowboy into a Prince ... 95

Etiquette: Ladies Are Mindful ... 103

Afterword ... 111

About the Author ... 113

Acknowldegements

First, my wonderful mother who has sacrificed for me and has been right by my side for the entirety of my journey. You are an amazing woman, mother, grandmother, friend, and a blessing who traveled with me and cared for Kayla while I poured into others. You believe in me and allow me to pursue my passions and purpose every day. I pray God's blessings rain down on you one hundred million-fold for what you have done for us. Your grace, poise, and love for us are true examples for me to follow.

My Auntie Tresa who has been one of my best supporters: you have consistently contributed to my success in business and my personal life. From giving me money or just a quiet place to rest, I cannot thank you enough.

My best friend Jenita, who is truly my reward from God. You have been a great friend to me and have taught me so much in the last six years. Your wisdom has guided me right back to the line, and I am confident that, because of you, I can wake up when the trumpet sounds. (Insider)

My business coach, Aprille Franks-Hunt: you never stopped believing in me and my ability to change the world on my own terms and on my own level. You have introduced me to my resilience and, for that, I am so grateful. Thank you for the hard talks, for Serendipity, for Ign!te, and for being a living example of a servant leader.

Ethel "Auntie Terrell" Marrache, Emril "Mecie" Johnson, Natalie Owens, Adriane McIntyre, Angel Brown, Angela Gibson-Shaw, Annay Herrera, Arlene Jackson, Uyonna Hill, Cherrie Johnson,

Dawniel Winningham, Diane Jones, Regina Thompson, Donna Oats, Ebony Combs, Essence Wilson, Jennifer Fontanilla, Kamilah Aquil, Mai Brooks, Makeda Smith, Reba Robinson, "Life Support Sisters", Mrs. Idella, Trayona Childress, Portasha Moore, Sharron Burrell, Shawntae "Fun Size" Sanders, Tamora Johnson, Varian Brown, Tierra Destiny Reid, Charease Richards, Tamargo "Boogie" Pleasant and Sharon Cruse: I want to thank you all for teaching me, listening to me, chin-checking me, loving me, pouring into me, and praying for me. For being the village that Kayla and I needed, exposing me to new levels and experiences, and investing in me. You all have allowed me to be vulnerable, and you have been trustworthy with that vulnerability. For being authentic, riding with me, riding for me, being a part of my growth, caring about my health, and allowing me to share my journey. For being great wives and mothers. For being my family and for reminding me that Kayla is always watching me. For demanding that I walk in integrity. For our talks, hugs, and tears. For Serendipity. For taking care of my daughter while I pursue my dreams. For being women I can trust. I love you all!

Purposely Created Team! Tieshena, you and your squad are amazing and I am grateful to you for believing in me and going above and beyond to help me make this dream become a reality. Your professionalism, kind hearts, and encouragement are priceless.

My Aunt Tamara "Cha-Cha" Shaw-Hunt who told me I was going to be a best-selling author years ago: I miss you so much. I know you would have come from whatever city, state, or country you would have been in to hug me and declare your pride. I miss our calls for my "wins" and I cherish your advice and legacy. I wish you were here to share this with me, but you live on in my heart and memories.

Special Thank You

Stephanie Sokol
A Total Woman
www.ATotalWoman.com
12743 Valley View Ave. La Mirada, CA 90638
562-404-9440
Chapter 2 Expert

Dr. Romeo Brooks
Roots Nutrition
www.rootsnutrition.com
1210 N. La Brea Ave, Inglewood, CA 90302
310-419-0835
Chapter 3 Expert

Donta Morrison
6in10.org
www.6in10.org
www.DontaMorrison.com
323-451-1496
Chapter 4 Expert

Special Thank You

SCHOOLS AND ORGANIZATIONS

Crenshaw High School

Centennial High School

Lifeline Charter High School

Dorsey High School

Montebello High School

Washington Preparatory High School

Pomona High School

TEACH Tech High School

Pennacle Foundation

Dream Catchers Foundation

Los Padrinos Juvenile Facility

Challengers Boys and Girls Club

Center for Youth and Family Collaborative

Department of Children and Family Services

Purple Reign Life Skills Center

After School All-Stars Los Angeles

Los Angeles Sparks

Los Angeles African American Women's Public Policy Institute

Foreword

In my years as a publicist, I have helped many clients achieve success in their businesses. And just as often, I saw some of these same clients struggle to achieve success in building strong relationships with their teenage daughters. As they grappled to help their teens transition into adulthood, I noticed that, for some, there was a lack of basic fundamentals. Those missing pieces are investigated in Kiana Shaw's book—these chapters have been great guides for me as a mom, aunt, and big sister to many young ladies.

When I met Kiana, she was serving girls in the inner city, openly sharing her past struggles in classrooms and on stages throughout Los Angeles County, and informing them about life, leadership, and empowerment. I was blown away by her ability to both effectively and affectively communicate with the girls and gain immediate results. Additionally, her ability to bring love, joy, and harmony to biological and blended families, as well as to schools, is nothing short of phenomenal. It is only fitting that she create a book to serve as an extension of her services.

This is the kind of advice I would want the young ladies in my life to get. It rings with the tone of a loving auntie who gets straight to the point about the realities of life while allowing you to rest on her shoulder. This book is priceless and timeless.

Monique Jackson
CEO of MomMeMogul, Inc.
Co-Founder of The GIMA Group

Preface

We've all had those talks: those uncomfortable parent to teenage girl conversations about sex, hygiene, social media, and other awkward topics that end with everyone looking at the floor and saying a quick, "Okay, great. Glad we had this talk. Bye." I Choose to be a Lady is a guide that helps avoid those moments and is meant for parents who want to communicate with and understand their teens and for girls who don't want to ask their parents questions, but need a trustworthy source to refer to.

I am proud of this piece of work and am excited to present it to you for your personal library. This book was designed to be your reference source for years to come. As you read through it, be sure to complete the chapter review questions and take notes on the pages provided. You will be able to go through this book again at a later date and see your growth. I truly believe every teenage girl should have her own copy of it.

Thank you for trusting me with your personal development.

CHAPTER ONE

What Is a Lady: Why Would I Want to Be One?

If you're anything like me, right around the age of five, you started wondering: what is a lady and why do they keep telling me to be one? Growing up, I had two brothers who spent a lot of time outdoors and I enjoyed being with them. We would hop fences, climb trees, race, and play football in the streets; those were the best times of my childhood. However, I was always told that I needed to act like a lady, sit like a lady, *be a lady*, and it never really made sense to me. It actually seemed quite boring, because, in my mind, being a lady meant big dresses, cooking, cleaning, and serving people.

It wasn't until I got older that I understood: a lady is elegant, cultured, considerate, courteous, helpful, peaceful, trustworthy, respectful, and well spoken. She also has good table manners, willingly compliments others, and practices great hygiene habits. A lady is protective of her body and personal brand. She gives from the heart. She is a peacemaker and peace-seeker. She is loyal, has strong opinions, and is a good sport who always seeks to grow and mature. These are some of the characteristics that I see in my own mother, aunts, and mentors, as well as women I admire from afar, such as Oprah Winfrey and Michelle Obama.

Now, if you discover that you don't possess the qualities mentioned above, don't worry! While some of these qualities have been instilled in you, others will be developed over time, naturally or with the help and guidance of a mentor.

Oftentimes, society paints a negative picture of what a lady is and how she behaves. With words like "prude," "prissy," and "goody-two shoes" being used, the lady is seen as weak because she does not involve herself in social media arguments, frivolous fights, and conversations about others. She respects her marriage and is loyal to her husband. Society sometimes even paints her as an oppressed doormat who is inferior to her male counterparts. But I have good news! A lady is not oppressed, brainless, or thoughtless. She is not inferior. She is not a gossip. She is not a "trap queen." She doesn't twerk for the public enjoyment of others nor is she interested in public humiliation. She isn't messy. She's not a bully in the cyber world or in person. Everything she does is calculated. She can contribute to great conversations and pioneer world-changing activities. She *is* the world changer.

Men react to ladies in a different way, with more positivity and humility, because the presence of a lady inspires an elevated level of respect. Ladies stand out. There is something special about a woman whose existence brings love, joy, peace, and other positive feelings, just by being in the room. She makes a dull meeting fun, a sad friend feel better, and makes everyone in the room feel loved.

REVIEW QUESTIONS

Chapter One
What is a Lady? Why Would I Want To Be One?

1. Name five characteristics of a lady. _____

   _____   _____

   _____   _____

2. Name two activities ladies don't indulge in.

   _____   _____

3. Fill in the blanks: Men react to ladies in a more

   _____, even more _____ way.

4. Fill in the blanks: The _____ of a lady _____ a level of _____ that being in the presence of other _____ does not.

Notes

CHAPTER TWO

Feminine Hygiene: Ladies Leave Behind a Scent, Not an Odor

If you have ever had an embarrassing moment for not smelling that great or your clothes being noticeably dirty, you probably realized that you have to be more intentional about keeping yourself clean. Offensive odors and un-kept hair can quickly give you the reputation of being "nasty" and create uncomfortable environments in which you might be teased. It's important for a young lady to develop the practice of great hygiene early.

Great hygiene is one of your first accomplishments in life. When you took the baby wipe from your mother and proudly proclaimed, "Mommy, I will do it myself," *that* was your first step. Going from diapers to pull-ups to panties and learning how to properly wipe yourself and wash your hands were all accomplishments.

Poor hygiene may have others see you as being lazy, dirty, and undisciplined. Dating, having friends, or getting hired for a job may become difficult, since people often have high expectations for hygiene. It is important to keep your body clean and your clothes fresh. This is the most basic area of femininity. Many young ladies in more disadvantaged or underserved areas around the world do not have the basic luxuries of showering, brushing their teeth, or washing their hair with shampoo. Others have access, but don't know how to properly make use of it all because they haven't been taught how.

Here are some things you can do to improve your hygiene and take care of both your body and mind:

Bathing

Did you know that you can smell bad and not know it? It's true. We're so familiar with our own body odors that we may not be aware of how we smell to others. Have you ever walked into someone's home and it has an odor to you, but the occupants don't seem to notice it? By the time we become aware of our smell, others have already gotten a whiff.

To cleanse your body, start with the water as warm as you can stand it. Let it completely rinse your entire body before using a washcloth, sponge, or loofa to add your soap. Gently scrub your entire body in a circular motion before rinsing with warm water. Then repeat. Be sure to wash your body at least twice during your time of menstruation, because your hormones are behaving differently at that time. Be sure to rinse your vaginal region thoroughly after washing to remove all soap, because soap buildup can cause you to itch.

If you play sports or other physical activities, be sure to bathe after practice and after games. Sometimes that will mean multiple showers in the same day.

Cleaning Your Underclothes

Wearing dirty underclothes contributes to poor hygiene. Some young ladies believe it's fine to wear underclothes, particularly bras, for several days in a row without changing them. Because they can't be seen, they don't think anyone can tell if they are not clean. However, underclothes are the closest garments to your body and they have a language of their own. They absorb sweat, discharges, body oils, and odors first. Others might not be able to *see* your underclothes, but that does not mean they cannot *smell* them.

Under shirts, socks and panties should be washed after each use. Bras should be changed every day, hand washed every few uses, and hung up to air dry so they don't lose their elasticity.

Hair

Depending on the texture and length, your hair should be shampooed once daily or perhaps once every two weeks. Keeping your hair clean will often help reduce acne and bad odors from product buildup and sweat. Keep in mind that everything in the air gets trapped in our hair every day. If you live in a smog-filled city like Los Angeles or near construction sites or farms, those places make a difference in how often you should shampoo your hair.

If you use a headscarf at night to wrap your hair up to keep it nice and neat for the next day, be sure that you wash the scarf at least once a week. If you just rest your head directly on pillowcases, make sure that you wash your pillowcases at least once a week because everything that's in your hair gets on there and your face touches them as well. While we're talking about pillowcases, let's also be sure to change our sheets once a week. I will explain more about this when we talk about the body.

Oily Hair

The hormones that create acne are the same ones that can make your hair feel like your mechanic used your ponytail to clean up motor oil. Each strand of hair has its own oil gland, which keeps the hair moisturized and shiny. During puberty, when the glands produce extra oil, your hair can look lackluster, oily, and greasy.

Dozens of shampoos are available in beauty supply stores, drugstores, and supermarkets for you to choose from. Most brands are pretty similar, although you want to try one that is specifically formulated for your hair type. Use warm water and a small amount of shampoo to work up a lather. Don't scrub or rub so hard that it irritates the scalp or damages your hair. After you have rinsed, you can follow up with a conditioner if you like; again, one for your hair type and texture will work best.

Face

Washing your face is an integral part of hygiene because our faces are the most exposed parts of our bodies. We often touch our faces with our hands, not realizing that our hands are unclean. When we hug other people, their hair and clothing touches our faces too. Add being kissed on our cheeks, the amount of sweat we produce, exercise, and all of the pollutants in our atmosphere, it is easy to see how our faces can be the dirtiest parts of our bodies at the end of the day. If you play sports, you should wash your face in the morning, after sports, and before bed. If you do not play a sport, you should at least wash your face when you wake up and before bed.

Eyes

Clean out your eyes. As a young lady, you want to be sure that, when people are looking into your eyes, they're not focusing on crust or "eye boogers." Your eyes should be crystal clear and ready for the world (and you should get at least eight hours of sleep daily, which aids in the prevention of red, irritated eyes!).

Nose
Our noses provide us with our sense of smell, but can also be great vacuums for allergies. To make sure your nose is working at its maximum capacity, you want to be sure you are blowing it every day and using a Q-tip, tissue, or towel to clean the insides. The hairs in your nose are there to protect you by trapping dust and dirt that might go into your lungs, and cause allergies, sneezing, and even colds. Use a tissue on your pinky finger to get into your nose and wipe the hairs clean.

Oral Hygiene
Oral care is extremely important. People can smell your breath at a distance the same way they can smell your body funk. Be sure to brush your teeth for at least two minutes, twice a day. Get a travel size toothbrush and toothpaste so you can brush after each meal. Be sure to floss in between each tooth, getting the back of your teeth and then smelling your dental floss. If it doesn't smell good to you, your breath doesn't smell good to anyone else. After you have brushed and flossed, use an antiseptic like Listerine, Scope, or even peroxide to rinse your mouth.

> ***Tip: Improve the brightness of your teeth by dipping your toothbrush in baking soda and brushing. Follow it up with your regular brushing routine. Do this weekly.

Ears
An often over-looked area when dealing with hygiene is our ears. Behind our ears is where our soap and hair products build up, so we must take special care of that area. Also, be sure to get inside of your ears and wipe all the way around. We naturally produce varied

amounts of earwax, and often, it is runny and must be cleaned out every day.

Additionally, if you have pierced ears, you want to make sure you don't use anyone else's earrings without sterilizing them first.

Neck

Be sure to use a towel or facial cleansing cloth to wash your neck, starting under your chin and then moving beneath and behind the ears. Rinse properly as soap can build there and give the appearance of dirt.

Underarms

Underarms produce a musty smell that can stop people in their tracks. Taking the time to bathe and wash your underarms with hot, soapy water is essential to maintaining good hygiene during the day. Be sure to use an antiperspirant to prevent sweating and stay fresh versus a deodorant that lingers over the odor the way air freshener does when sprayed in a room that already smells bad.

> ****Tip: If you are out of antiperspirant, you can take a small amount of baking soda, make a little paste out of it, and rub that under your arms. Another option is to cut a raw potato or a lemon and rub a slice under your arms. If you have recently shaved, choose the potato instead of the lemon so the citrus doesn't sting your skin. I promise you won't smell like french fries. Just remember that these are temporary options to antiperspirant and are not intended for long-term use.*

Breasts

Depending on their size, your breasts may get damp, particularly in the cleavage or underneath. Wash and swipe your antiperspirant in those areas to prevent them from getting musty and chaffing, especially during the summer months.

Often times, we forget to wash our bras or change them out, and, as a result, our breasts may become itchy or irritated from sweat or un-rinsed soap. To solve that problem, wash and rinse your bras properly every few uses and don't wear one more than two days in a row.

Navel

More and more I see bellybuttons/navels being exposed in outfits. If you follow this trend, make sure you use a towel while you're in the shower to clean your navel. When you're done, put a little bit of alcohol on a cotton ball and rub the inside of your bellybutton.

Toes

Our feet are enclosed in shoes most of the day and they accumulate sweat, so we want to be sure we are changing our socks every day. Adding a little baking soda inside your shoes will help absorb odors. If you don't have baking soda, try a little baby powder to absorb sweat.

Cleaning underneath and between your toenails should also be a daily ritual to prevent smelly feet. Clean them out and wipe whatever you clean off onto a paper towel or a piece of toilet paper that can be thrown away immediately. Whatever you do, don't wipe your toe jam on your bed's comforter or the floor.

Genitalia

Our genitalia and anus can be the source of some of our bodies' most offensive smells. Puberty exacerbates this fact. Cleansing your vagina and anus is not optional—it's mandatory. Taking hot, soapy showers every day as well as changing your panties, using panty liners, and wiping from vagina to anus correctly every time you use the bathroom, are all great defenses against bad hygiene. During menstruation or your period when your body discharges blood from your uterus, you need to take special care to clean your genitalia sometimes twice daily to prevent offensive odors.

Puberty causes all kinds of changes in your body. Every day it seems like you have new hair growing in different places, some of which may make you uncomfortable. At times, you may sweat for no reason; then, you'll notice that there are odors where you never had them before.

Body Hair

Body hair in new places is something you can count on—again, it's hormones in action. You may decide to leave the hair on your legs and underarms as is or you may shave them. It's your choice whether to shave or not, just be sure to talk to your parent or guardian first if you are under eighteen.

If you do decide to shave, you have a few choices: you can use a traditional razor with shaving cream or gel or an electric razor. If you use a regular razor, make sure the blade is new and sharp to prevent cuts and nicks. Shaving creams and gels are often a better choice than soap, because they make it easier to glide the razor against your skin. Some of the newer razors contain shaving gel right in the blade area, making beginners feel comfortable shaving.

Whether you're shaving your legs or armpits, go slowly. These are tricky areas of your body with lots of curves and angles, and it's easy to cut yourself if you move too fast.

Shaving Your "Other" Hair

Although it may not appear to be so, pubic hair removal irritates and inflames the hair follicles left behind, leaving very small open wounds that can barely be seen. Once you start shaving your pubic hair, frequent hair removal is necessary to stay smooth, which may mean that the shaved or waxed area is irritated on a regular basis. When that irritation is combined with the warm moist environment of the vagina, it becomes a prime breeding ground for bacterial diseases, such as staph boils and abscesses that a doctor must cut and drain to avoid further infection. It is very common to find puss filled pimples and other hair-follicle blisters in the genital area.

Furthermore, clinicians are finding that freshly shaved pubic areas and genitals are also more vulnerable to herpes infections due to the microscopic wounds being exposed to viruses carried by the mouth or genitals, as well as other STI's. In addition, when your pubic hair grows back, the skin may be irritated and itchy. Be mindful of where you are when you scratch.

Pubic hair is nothing to be embarrassed about. Its purpose is to provide a cushion against friction that can cause skin abrasions and injuries, as well as to protect you from bacteria and other unwanted pathogens. It is also a badge of honor for some since it is the visible result of successfully passing through adolescence.

Acne

Acne is another visible sign that you have entered the adolescent phase of life. Acne occurs when your oil glands, which lubricate your hair and skin, become stimulated by your hormones and overproduce oil that clog pores. It is a skin condition that usually shows up on the face, neck, shoulders, upper back, and chest as **pimples** (the wall of the pore opens, allowing oil, bacteria, and dead skin cells to make their way under the skin), **blackheads** (a pore gets clogged up, but stays open and the top surface darkens), **whiteheads** (a pore gets clogged up and closes, but bulges out from the skin), or **cysts** (closed pockets of tissue that can be filled with fluid, pus, or other material). 80% of teens have recurring acne, but knowing this fact certainly never helped me when I was staring at pimples on my own face while getting ready for school. Let's talk about the causes of these pimples and what you can do about them.

Wash your face twice a day to help prevent oil buildup that contributes to acne. If you are active in sports or exercise every day, be sure to wash your face after these activities, because sweat makes your face like a sticky pad that collects everything in the air. You may be tempted to scrub your face, but don't do that—acne can't be scrubbed away. Irritating the skin and pores may actually worsen your condition. Be as gentle as you can.

Many over-the-counter lotions and creams containing salicylic acid or benzyl peroxide are available to help prevent and clear up acne. Follow the directions on the product to avoid drying out your skin and causing your oil glands to start overproducing oil in response. Your skin can end up looking worse.

Here are a few more tips:

- Don't pop pimples: It's tempting, but popping them can push infected material further into the skin, leading to more swelling, redness, and even scarring.

- Wash your hands before applying anything to your face, such as moisturizers and makeup, and always avoid touching your face with your fingers. Your hands are dirty, because you touch doorknobs, desks, chairs and counters, and so on all day. You are putting the germs from each of those things onto your face.

- Wipe off your phone and glasses often, because they collect the oils from your face.

- Remove your makeup before you go to sleep and throw away any makeup that smells or looks different from when you first bought it.

- Shampoo your hair often and keep it off of your face to prevent additional dirt and oil from clogging your pores.

Sweat and Body Odor

Sweat comes from glands we have all over our bodies, which become hyper active during puberty and begin releasing different chemicals. This results in sweat with stronger odors, especially in your armpits, feet, and genitalia.

The best thing to do is to bathe every day, washing away any bacteria that contribute to the smells. Be mindful to wear clean clothes, t-shirts, socks, and underwear made from cotton or other natural materials to help absorb sweat more effectively.

Menstruation

The female body is different than the male body because of its ability to reproduce. The genital area during menstruation requires special care and consideration. Failure to carefully and properly care for your body during this time is a straight shot to poor hygiene. If your vagina is not kept clean, it will emit a foul, musty odor that is impossible to cover up, and this can be very embarrassing. It is a telltale sign to those who come in contact with you that you do not properly care for yourself.

During your menstrual cycle, you may want to take more than one shower per day and take special care during the day to not leave a foul smell behind. You can carry baby wipes, which come in very thin portable containers, and after using the bathroom and wiping the way you normally would, take the disposable wipes and freshen up your genitals area. You can also carry a small bag of baking soda with you, so when you change your Kotex, you can sprinkle a little baking soda onto it to help absorb the smell. Even when you are not menstruating, you can use panty liners to help absorb the odor and the vaginal fluids that secrete into your underwear.

Mark your calendar each month, but at first, you will need to be sure what your cycle will be. Some girls' menstrual cycles come every twenty-eight days while others come every forty days. The important thing is to know your body's cycle, when you are going to start and how this can vary from month-to-month. However, you do want to make sure that you have something on your calendar so that you can start to plan for your cycle whenever it does come. All of our bodies function differently. The period could last between seven and ten days, sometimes more. Many women also have three to five-day periods. Pay attention to your body. Be prepared.

Once your menstrual cycle begins, your body also produces female hormones estrogen and progesterone. Changes in these hormones can cause feelings that, together, are called premenstrual syndrome or PMS. Some girls have painful cramps in their stomachs, headaches, mood swings, or cravings for certain foods right before their periods begin. During this time, the body may retain water, which can make a girl feel puffy and bloated. Rings and shoes may feel tight at this time.

Bras

Finding a good bra can be difficult, especially if you are larger than a D cup. The most important thing to remember is that there are two parts to bra sizing: the chest size, which measures your back, and the cup size of your breast. You must get both measured to ensure a proper fit. If a lady wears a bra that's too big or loose around the ribcage, the band will ride up her back and her breasts will dump in the front, which can cause her to look larger or heavier. Big bras can also wrinkle and pucker, which doesn't look good under clothes. Bras that are too small in the cup will compress the breasts and force them to bulge out the sides (think armpit boobs). I suggest getting yourself professionally measured, but you can always calculate your chest and cup measurements yourself. All you need is a measuring tape.

Chest Measurement

Bra fitting experts offer a couple of methods of calculating the chest measurement, but the most common method involves running a tape measure just *under* your breasts, all the way around your back and ribcage. The tape measure should rest flat on your skin and lie straight across your back—not so tight that it digs in, but not so loose that it sags down in back. Make a note of your measurement and add five inches. This is your chest size.

If your chest measurement comes out as an odd number such as 31 or 33 inches, it's usually a good rule to round up to the next number. Bras tend to stretch over time and most bras have a few sets of adjustable hooks and eyes, so you can adjust the tightness. Pay attention to the fabric of the bras as well. Some are made of materials that stretch and you can fit more of your breast into a cup that stretches.

Cup Measurement

As with the chest measurement, when you are measuring for cup size, make sure the tape is not too loose or too tight. If you already own an unpadded bra that fits well, wear it when measuring for cup size. But be careful about the type of bra you wear to take your measurements—sports bras can flatten breasts and give a cup reading that's too small and padded, while lined bras have the opposite effect.

This time, when you run the tape measure around your body, you're going to take the measurement across the *fullest* part of your breasts. Write down this number and subtract your chest measurement. If the difference between the two numbers is less than one inch, your cup size is AA. If it is one inch, your cup size is A; two inches, you are a B cup; three inches you are a C cup, and so on.

Different brands and styles of bras will fit differently. Remember to bring several options with you into the dressing room. Before you put your clothes back on to go out of the dressing room and look for a different size, experiment by making some adjustments to your current bra. If the bra has an adjustable closure, extend or shorten the band slightly by moving the hooks to a different spot or adjusting the Velcro if the bra has that type of closing. The bottom band of a properly fitting bra should ride across the middle of your back and pass under your shoulder blades to provide the right support.

A bra's straps allow you to modify how the cups fit and support your breasts. When the straps are the right length, a bra lifts the breasts comfortably and the back of the bra will run straight across your back (if a bra is pulling upward in the back, it may be a sign that the straps are too tight). You should be able to get one finger under the straps to prevent them from digging into your shoulders. In general, girls who are petite will need to wear their bra straps shorter than girls who are taller. If you've made the straps looser and they are still digging into your shoulders, the cup size might be too small for you.

The cups also might be too small if you notice your breasts bulging out the sides, top, or bottom of the bra. If you notice that the cups are puckering or that there is a gap between your breasts and the bra, the cups are too big.

What Causes Breast Tenderness?

One of the most common times breasts might feel tender is when they are beginning to develop. First, you might notice a small button-like lump beneath the nipple area. The medical name for this is the breast bud and it is often present in both boys and girls. The breast bud may be a little tender and may cause you to worry, but it's a normal part of puberty. It is also common to have sore breasts around the beginning of your menstruation.

Just as armpits and feet sweat, so can breasts. All of that retained fluid forces the breast tissue to expand, which makes breasts feel achy or tender. Ask your parents for a pain reliever if you need it. Also, try cutting down on salty foods and foods that contain caffeine like coffee, tea, and chocolate.

Other Points to Remember

Please remember that hygiene is not solely about your body: it's also about your living space. Having dirty clothes on the floor makes your room smell. Having large amounts of dirty clothes in a hamper can also make your room smell. Be sure to pick up your clothing daily, put them in the proper place, wash them often, put your shoes away, and have a clear open space every day. Your bedroom trash should be emptied daily.

If you have a car, be sure to clean it out weekly. Hang a small grocery bag around the gearshift or put it in your side holder so you can throw trash away immediately. Remove clothing, papers, and books, and be sure to vacuum the inside as well as wash the outside of your car when needed.

The most important reason for practicing good hygiene is *you*. Un-cleanliness can become a health issue and can certainly contribute to lowered self-esteem. Here are some additional tools to aid in your feminine hygiene:

- Panty liners
- Shampoo
- Conditioner
- Sanitary pads
- Dental floss
- Mouthwash
- Soaps
- Perfumes
- Toothbrush
- Toothbrush holder
- Feminine wipes
- Antiperspirants
- Lotions
- Powder
- Facial cleanser
- Baking soda
- Nail clippers
- Nail brush
- Q-Tips
- Cotton balls
- Boar bristle brush

REVIEW QUESTIONS

Chapter Two
Feminine Hygiene: Ladies Leave Behind
a Scent, Not an Odor

1. Why is it important to be sure to rinse your vaginal area thoroughly after washing it? _____
_____

2. How often should you shampoo your hair?
_____

3. How often should you wash your face?
_____

4. If deodorant is not available, what can you use as a substitute for it?
_____

5. What can you use to prevent chaffing under your breast?
_____

6. What's the best way to clean your bellybutton?
_____

7. How often should you bathe if you have sports practice after school?

   _____

8. During your menstruation, what is a way to combat odor?

   _____

9. After using the restroom, what is the correct way to wipe yourself?

   _____

Notes

Controlling Your Weight: Ladies Know They Are More Than a Number on a Scale

So often, I hear people talking about weight loss and weight gain. Since there are so many myths about controlling our weight, I called Dr. Romeo Brooks, founder of *Roots Nutrition*, here in Los Angeles, to help us understand more on this subject.

Family Genetics

I told Dr. Brooks about a book I was reading that said family genetics play a big role in whether an individual will end up becoming fat or skinny. The book basically blamed our God-given DNA for our weight challenges, pretty much saying, "If your parents are fat, you will be fat too."

Dr. Brooks laughed a little and said, "No, that's not true. That's definitely a generalization. If you're fat, you're fat for a reason. Your body is intelligent. Genetics do play a role because your cells, like you, eat, drink, breathe, excrete waste, get excited, etc. They have memory and imagination and they make deliberate decisions. They are the reason why you look like your parents on the outside, physically. And because of your cellular structure, you look like them on the inside as well.

"As it relates to weight, health, and bodies, you can change the memory of a cell. Genetics and cellular memory play a role, but they don't determine it. You must listen to what the body is saying. The person is fat, which is an effect. You've got to go to a cause, and if you remove the cause, it doesn't matter what your genetic disposition is. People in a family have the tendency to eat the same way so their recipes and food choices are hereditary, not their fat. Soul food, for instance, predisposes us to diabetes. It makes our blood like syrup because the sugar in it makes it so thick that it doesn't move through our limbs. So our great grandparents, grandparents, and parents all make the same foods and we continue passing this on to our children. We make it, eat it, and, even though we see the complications it causes, we eat it while discussing how it is killing us. It is a diabetic meal. That's why we fall asleep right afterward. The acid in the food gets into your bloodstream, and this is what makes us lethargic."

Eat Better

Eating better may not be as convenient as eating junk food, but it isn't much harder to do. Dr. Brooks suggests that you identify the vegetables you like and eat them: "Eat your uncooked vegetables first, then the cooked vegetables to displace what's in your stomach, so you automatically eat less acidic foods. You want to eat more alkaline-forming foods compared to acid-forming foods. That's the reason why we're overweight. The acids we consume in our foods cause our bodies to produce more fat as a defense mechanism."

In his book *Stop Hiding the Fat,* Dr. Brooks writes about the cause and effects of fat in our bodies, specifically noting this acid. "Your fat has been protecting and defending you in its pursuit to maintain your life. Fat is deliberately created by the body to keep the acid in check," he writes. "The over-production of acid produced by our acid-based diets sends the body into a frenzy to protect itself from the harmful effects of the acid. And while some acid is evacuated through the bowel, the bladder, the lungs, and the skin, what is left in the body must be buffered and neutralized."

An overabundance of acid in the body is harsh and abrasive; plus, it burns. When acid is produced beyond its tolerance level, the body does several things to protect itself:

1. Retains water to dilute the acid, creating inflammation.
2. Produces cholesterol to protect the blood vessels from the acid, developing high cholesterol.
3. Uses calcium and other alkaline minerals to neutralize the acid, creating porous bones or osteoporosis.
4. Produces fat to buffer and store the acid, adding excess fat.

However, fat is not necessarily all bad: Dr. Brooks went on to explain to me that "without these defense mechanisms in place, cells, tissues, and organs would deteriorate faster than the body can repair them, and you would die. Fat production is a life-saving effort on the body's part that aims at self-preservation and vitality. The amount of fat that is produced in your body is indicative of the amount of acid that threatens your life."

Eat Alkaline Foods

We've now learned that fat is your body's defense mechanism against organ failure. As soon as you alkalize your body by consuming alkaline foods such as raw fruits and vegetables and juices, the fat leaves. Eating alkaline foods is your offense to great health.

Dr. Brooks says, "It takes four parts alkaline to neutralize one part acid. So, the thing is, you've got to balance it out. Most of us have an acidic diet. We eat buffalo wings, meatballs, or pizza, and no vegetables. Our body is 72 percent water. How many high water content foods do we eat? Let breakfast be raw, then eat a big salad before lunch and dinner."

Estrogen

Estrogen is an acidic hormone both males and females produce, although women produce more of it; that's the reason why women usually have more fat than men. Dr. Brooks notes, "Young women are becoming estrogen dominant earlier because they are ingesting estrogen by consuming the hormones from animals' byproducts which explains why girls are starting their periods earlier than ever. Hormones need to be balanced and the imbalance women are experiencing is causing fibroids, endometriosis, ovarian cysts and fibrosis breasts."

Cellulite

Cellulite is a part of your body's connective tissue and it's not just evident on larger people—you can be skinny and have it. As Dr. Brooks explains, "Think of a ball of cotton candy like it's fat. When you grab it in the middle with both hands and squeeze it, you're going to have this dimpling effect." He also suggests jump roping and, again, consuming more live fruits and vegetables as the best ways to get rid of cellulite.

Stress

Stress is created by thoughts. When we dwell on those thoughts, our bodies become acidic and we tend to eat more of the foods that are high in fat and create more acid. Our bodies' responses to what we put inside and on top of ourselves are visible barometers for what is occurring to us mentally, emotionally, and spiritually.

Remember: fat is created to alkalize our bodies and save our lives!

Acid

Over-production of acid as a result of stress can literally burn a hole in your gut—this is called gastritis. Acid in the small intestine is called enteritis, while acid in the colon is called colitis. "What is '-itis?' Inflammation," Dr. Brooks says. "Why do you have 'inflammation'? Because, acid is a fire. When your body sends the water to the fire to put it out, you get inflamed. You swell up. The body always does what it needs to do."

Fat

I asked Dr. Brooks if we should try to get our body to 0 percent fat and he said, "You want fat. Fat is fuel, storage, warmth, and cushion for the body. You produce hormones with it. There are two kinds of fat, but only one is necessary:

1. Depot fat is all the excess that no one needs. This is the fat you have on your hips, thighs, belly, back of your arms, and back.
2. Subcutaneous fat is fat beneath the skin. This is essential fat. You need it for warmth and to cushion the organs.

Counting Calories

I once joined a weight loss program that had me counting calories for everything I ate, including gum. "Don't do that!" Dr. Brooks said. "It's too cerebral and intellectual. Eat when you're hungry, sleep when you're sleepy, play and run around. There is so much marketing that tells us to count calories, eat for your body type, eat for your blood type, eat more protein, eat fewer carbohydrates, or eat more carbohydrates. Some even say eat more fat. I say, eat raw plant foods."

Everything we need, all the nutrition, vitamins, and minerals, are in raw fruits and vegetables. Eat more raw foods with the cooked foods you eat and add an active lifestyle. That's the secret to weight loss.

Here is a list of some alkaline foods to get you started:

Fruits
- Apples
- Tomatoes
- Grapefruit
- Peaches
- Pineapples
- Cherries
- Apricots
- Strawberries
- Bananas
- Blueberries
- Pears
- Grapes
- Kiwis
- Melons
- Tangerines
- Figs
- Mangoes
- Papayas
- Lemons
- Limes

Veggies

- Corn
- Mushrooms
- Turnips
- Bell pepper
- Radish
- Avocados
- Lettuce
- Celery
- Cabbage
- Cauliflower
- Carrots
- Cucumbers
- Asparagus
- Kale
- Radish
- Collard greens
- Onions
- Sweet potatoes
- Eggplant
- Peas
- Green beans
- Beets
- Spinach
- Broccoli
- Artichoke
- Brussels sprouts

REVIEW QUESTIONS

Chapter Three
Controlling Your Weight: Ladies Know They
Are More Than a Number on a Scale

1. True or False:
   If your parents are overweight, naturally, you will be too.

2. True or False:
   Body fat is produced in defense of the acid we consume in our foods.

3. Name two things the body does to protect itself from an over abundance of acid:
   1. _____
   2. _____

4. How many parts of alkaline does it take to neutralized one part of acid?
   _____

5. Name five alkaline fruits: _____
   _____ _____
   _____ _____

6. Name five alkaline vegetables: _____
   _____ _____
   _____ _____

7. What are the two types of fats we have in our bodies?

   _____   _____

8. Of the two fats listed above, which one do we need?

   _____

9. Where can we find the best sources of our nutrition, vitamins, and minerals?

   _____ and _____

Notes

Sex: Ladies Make Informed Decisions About Sex

In most households, sex, as it relates to teenage girls, seems forbidden or, at best, a very uncomfortable subject. The adults have their own relationships with sexual activity, which usually determines how they speak about it. For instance, a father who was promiscuous as a teen will usually speak differently about sex with his son than another father who waited until marriage. In the same way, a mother who was sexually assaulted may view sex in her marriage as a service she performs for her husband and may only speak about it in this way. Meanwhile, another woman may have only experienced sex through the loving touches of her husband. She may be openly playful with her husband, touching frequently, and making flirty comments to let him know that she wants intimacy with him.

With that being said, an enormous consideration that a lady must take in having sex is sexually transmitted infections (STIs). Roughly half of sexually active teens in the United States will catch a sexually transmitted infection by the time they turn twenty-five, and yet, many know very little about STIs. Most young ladies haven't done any research on them outside of school assignments or until they become infected with one. Unfortunately, parents and schools don't always provide the information and resources needed to address this widespread issue. Over the years, I have been fortunate enough to offer hundreds of workshops with teenagers about sexual health and responsibility. Here, I have compiled the top ten questions that teenagers ask me during our workshops.

Question 1
How can I prevent STIs?

1. *Abstinence*: Hands down, it is the only way to guarantee protection.
2. *Condoms*: When used consistently and correctly for oral, anal, and vaginal intercourse, they are effective for preventing the majority of STIs.
3. *Monogamy*: That means you agree to be sexually active with only one person, who also agrees to be sexually active with only you. But always remember that you cannot control another person's actions and you can never be certain that your partner is being faithful.
4. *Be Informed and Smart*: If you or your partner has been diagnosed with an STD, you both need to get treated and re-tested and stop having sex until your doctor says you can resume. That way, the infection can clear out of both of you and you lessen the risk of passing it back to your partner. If only one of you gets treated or if one of you doesn't finish the prescribed medication, you *will* re-infect your partner.

5. *HPV vaccination*: I am not advocating this, just informing you. The human papilloma virus can be carried by both men and women cause warts on the skin, anal, and genital areas. It can also be the cause for cervical cancer in women. HPV is the most common sexually transmitted disease in the world for people between fifteen to twenty-four-years old. The vaccination does not prevent syphilis, gonorrhea, chlamydia, or the herpes virus, and vaccinated women should still practice protective sexual behavior.

Question 2
Do all condoms work against STIs?

The short answer is no. Let's talk about the types of condoms available:
1. *Latex*: The most commonly used form. When worn with every sexual encounter, consistently and correctly, it is highly effective at preventing STIs, including diseases transmitted by genital secretions and the sexual transmission of HIV.
2. *Polyurethane*: These condoms tend to be more expensive, but it needs to be used by people who are allergic to latex. They are very effective forms of protection, but they're not as widely available.
3. *Female*: Also made of polyurethane and works very well when used correctly. The opening gives you more protection against skin-to-skin contact and it helps to prevent the spread of genital herpes. *Do not* use it while also using a male condom, because the friction of the two rubbing against one another will create holes in the material.

4. Lamb skin: This natural-skin condom is usually preferred by people who seek heightened sensitivity. However, viruses can get through some of the natural skin condoms' porous membrane. They should not be trusted unless you know your partner isn't having sex with anyone else.

It's important to put the condom on the second there's an erection. If you wait until after there's been a little grinding or even a little bit of penetration, you're putting yourself at risk, because there are pre-ejaculatory fluids that can be unconstrained and can cause both STIs and unplanned pregnancies. On my YouTube channel, www.youtube.com/CoachKianaShaw, you can watch the video I created to show you how to properly put on a condom, how to use a female condom, and how to create a dental dam. You can also consult your health care provider, school nurse, local clinics, as well as reference educational materials about safe sex practices.

Question 3
Is there a way to tell if my partner has an STD without going to the doctor?

No. Many people think that they can look at a person and know if they have an infection. Unfortunately, it's not that easy. Chlamydia causes a white discharge in women and clear discharge in men that looks like pre-ejaculation fluid. Syphilis causes a clear discharge and chancre sores to develop on the genitals. Gonorrhea causes a yellowish, cloudy discharge accompanied by painful urination. In many women, gonorrhea and chlamydia only cause odors and no other symptoms.

With all that being said, most of these STIs are what we call asymptomatic, meaning they have no symptoms at all. Herpes is spreading amongst our teens like wildfire, not because they see blisters on their partner's genital area and say, "I want blisters too!" but because it doesn't always show signs. The only way to be sure is to go to a doctor and get tested.

Question 4
Will the clinic I go to tell my parents if I get tested?

No. Privacy is one of the major concerns teens have about accessing care. The majority of states have laws that permit teens to obtain reproductive health services for contraception and STD testing, diagnosis, and treatment without their parent's consent. However, every state has its own polices on this, so inform yourself about your state's laws.

Question 5
Which STIs should I be tested for?

I recommend that all sexually active teenagers get tested for chlamydia, syphilis, and gonorrhea every year. I also strongly advocate that they get HIV tested every six months to a year, sometimes more frequently depending on their level of risk. Now, to some, this may sound excessive, but it takes three months for HIV to show up in your blood stream, and if you have multiple partners, you may end up blaming the wrong person and infecting someone else. Being honest about your sexual activity will help your healthcare provider decide how frequently you should be tested.

Now, syphilis is not that common in teenagers, but in Los Angeles, it is a real and existing problem for the teenage population. Be wise and get tested whether your partner tests positive for STIs or not.

Question 6
How are STI tests done?

Syphilis, gonorrhea, herpes, hepatitis B, and HIV are detected through blood draw tests, meaning that your blood needs to be taken with a needle. If you are having anal sex, there is an anal swab done for testing, and a throat culture if you are having oral sex. To be tested for chlamydia and gonorrhea, you must urinate in a cup for a urine test. For women: If you have pelvic pain or discharge, then you need to have a pelvic exam and a Pap smear. It's uncomfortable, but not necessarily painful.

Question 7
Will I have to get a shot if I have an STI?

There are several different antibiotics for treatable STIs caused by bacteria. A shot may be a preferred, quick and easy, somewhat painful option. The other option is to take medication for a period of time ranging from one dose to two weeks. Unfortunately, for viral STIs, there is no cure, only treatment to control your condition. If you become infected with herpes, it is a lifelong, chronic, viral infection that can only be medicated to help decrease the severity and duration of the symptoms. Once again, it will not cure you. Once you have it, it is there to stay.

Question 8
What is the best way to prevent pregnancy?

Abstinence. You may be tired of hearing this, but it is the only way to ensure one hundred percent safety against pregnancy and sexually transmitted infections. All other methods of birth control carry risks. Condoms, when used inconsistently or improperly, bring a relatively high danger of failure, and latex condoms are the only form of protection that can stop the transmission of HIV while preventing pregnancies. Remember that birth control pills, IUDs, diaphragms, and spermicides do not prevent HIV.

Question 9
Can I get an STI from oral or anal sex?

Absolutely. Oral sex is not safer sex. Giving and receiving oral sex can transmit STIs the same way intercourse can, because most of these viruses or bacteria enter the body through tiny cuts or mucous membranes during sex. Every form of sexual contact increases the chance of transmission. Herpes, syphilis, gonorrhea, HIV, hepatitis A, B, and C can all be transmitted through oral sex. Often times, we have tiny cuts in our mouths from something as simple as eating potato chips or brushing our teeth, and we don't even know that we've increased our chances of getting an STI. Condoms and dental dams can help reduce the risk of getting infected via oral sex: check out my YouTube channel at www.youtube.com/CoachKianaShaw for a video I produced on the subject.

Understand that any and every sexual encounter puts you at risk and the only way to be one hundred percent free from STIs is to not have sex until you are with a committed and trustworthy partner. Teens and young adults have the highest rates of infections of any age group and there are ten million new youth infections every year, the most common being HPV, affecting about 35 percent of fourteen to nineteen-year-olds.

Question 10
Should I talk to my partner about sexual activity if we are not having sex yet?

I saved this question for last, because it is asked so often and I want to be clear: if you are in a relationship, whether or not you're having sex, you should be discussing sex with your partner and asking questions about their sexual history for several reasons:
1. Establish sexual boundaries, meaning that you can decide how far you're willing to take the relationship sexually.
2. Discover if your partner has engaged in high-risk sex. You may learn if your partner enjoys sex with both men and women, if your partner previously engaged in sex without condoms, or if they have had pre-exposures to STIs. You want all that information.
3. Start or continue conversations about safe sex habits, which is definitely something you want to be upfront about.

Although talking about sex is crucial, remember that talking can't always help you determine if your partner has an STI. Even if they promise they are STI-free and sexually healthy, they may be infected and not know it. Once again, three-fourths of women and half of men who are infected with chlamydia have no symptoms. The only way to find out for sure is if you get tested.

Cold Sores

Cold sores usually show themselves as tender blisters on the lips caused by the herpes virus (HSV-1), so they *are* transmittable. Just like genital herpes, once you are infected with this virus, it stays in your body, resulting in cold sores throughout your life. However, cold sores usually go away on their own after a week or two. But if you get them often or they become a constant problem, talk to your doctor or dermatologist.

Here are some tips to prevent or decrease cold sores:

- Avoid sharing toothbrushes, drinks, lip balm, with other people.

- Eat well, exercise, use suntan lotion, and get plenty of sleep. Too much stress, sun, and illness can cause cold sores to flare up.

- Take pain medication if your cold sores are painful.

- Do not consume acidic foods like oranges and soda, because they can cause irritation.

- Don't pick at them! They will become infected with bacteria.

Final Thoughts

As a professional, I urge you to speak with your parents or another trusted adult about sex. Your peers are often inaccurate with their information, and even worse, they are the main source of pressure.

REVIEW QUESTIONS

Chapter Four
Sex: Ladies Make Informed Decisions About Sex

1. What are two ways to prevent Sexually Transmitted Infections?

   _____   _____

2. Name four types of condoms.

   _____   _____

   _____   _____

3. True or False:
   You can look at a person and tell if they have an STI.

4. Name two STIs sexually active teens should be tested for every year.

   _____   _____

5. True or False:
   Herpes is a bacterial disease.

6. True or False:
   The herpes infection can be cured.

7. What is the best way to prevent unwanted pregnancies?

   _____

8. True or False:
   Condoms always prevent pregnancy.

9. True or False:
   You can get an STI from oral and anal sex.

10. True or False:
    Herpes, syphilis, gonorrhea, HIV, hepatitis A, B, and C can all transmit through oral sex.

10. Why is it important to talk about sex with your partner even if you aren't sexually active?

_____

_____

_____

_____

_____

_____

_____

_____

Notes

CHAPTER FIVE

Self-Esteem:
Ladies Love Themselves First

Over the last six years, I have spent thousands of hours on school campuses throughout Los Angeles County. One of the skills I've developed in this time is my ability to identify teen girls with high, moderate, or low self-esteem.

Teens with moderate to low self-esteem are the bullies on campus. They are girls who can't make any moves by themselves and won't even go to the restroom without their BFFs. They are the girls who wear tight outfits, short skirts, short shorts, and often can't leave the house without any makeup. They are class clowns and attention/approval seekers. They are sore losers who *need* to be identified by their looks, athletic status, or some other way they deem credible. They are oftentimes promiscuous and rude.

I can also spot the kids who possess high self-esteem. They are focused, running for office, or in a leadership position somewhere in their lives. They walk to the beat of their own drum and don't follow the crowd, because they're independent thinkers—the crowd follows them. They don't spend time with negative people, they are comfortable being alone, and they make no apologies for being smart and successful. Yes, they may be athletes, but they know they are special off or on the field.

Another gift that I have is the ability to tell what a lady's self-esteem is based on her friends and her dates. Understanding what self-esteem is, identifying your own level, and healthily improving yourself are all essential to a great life.

Self-Esteem

Self-esteem is essentially how you feel about yourself. High or positive self-esteem means you love yourself, both inside and out. A common misconception is that self-esteem is based on how you physically look, but that isn't the whole of it. In fact, our self-esteem should not be tied to our weight, physical defects, or shoe sizes. Exaggerating your perceived flaws of height, weight, or complexion may be a sign that you need to work on how you see yourself. If you also think you are not smart enough and worthy of love (or better love), or barrage yourself with negative thoughts about your life, it's time to begin practicing positive affirmations.

It's easy to like who you are when you are winning. We all feel great when we get an A on our final exam, make the winning shot, or tell a funny joke that makes everyone laugh. How do you feel about yourself when you make a C, miss the final shot, or bomb out in the talent show? Your reactions and emotions will tell you where your self-esteem stands.

Being disappointed in yourself for your mistakes and failures doesn't mean you have low self-esteem. What matters is how you internalize those moments and project them into your overall life. Self-esteem is important because, as a teen, you are expected to know the difference between right and wrong and to, more often than not, choose the right. Positive self-esteem gives you the guts to be an independent thinker and make the right decisions when the pressure is on.

Peer pressure is probably something you face every day. Right now, you may desire or be urged to be a part of the "turn-up" crew, whether that's with the cheerleaders or band members. Belonging to a crowd is part of growing up—it helps you learn social skills, be a friend, discover your ability to be a leader, learn which people are bad, good, or great for you, and learn about the world around you. The key is to be authentic about who you are and understand that these relationships may be short-lived. It is perfectly natural to desire being liked by others, but not when it means you give into the negative pressures, even when they seem harmless.

Your friends are making a lot of their own choices regarding clothes, make up, sex, and other day-to-day issues, but their choices may or may not be good for you. For example, if you have friends who choose to study and keep their grades up or choose to spend time enjoying fun activities that do not involve sex, drugs, gangs, or alcohol, those are also great choices that can have a positive effect on you. Oppositely, if your friends are into mischievous activities, having mere associations can bring about devastating consequences. Knowing that an activity is wrong but still taking part in it just because your friends are doing it is a sign of low self-esteem. Remember: a lot of negativity is done in groups, but death, harm, and jail usually affects one person in the group more than the others.

Is Self-Esteem Learned or Given?

I often get asked if self-esteem is learned. To be honest, it's not that simple. High self-esteem is learned, and just like any skill, you have to put in practice to master it. Some people have trained themselves without even being aware of it. The end result is that they are confident, happy, and successful. With that being said, low self-esteem can also be a skill and a natural-born facet. You unknowingly practice being negative, and sadly, most of us have studied it for years. We live in defeat most of the time and never understand why. Go to www.KianaShaw.com to download my FREE Affirmations e-book.

Some argue that high self-esteem is also a natural gift. From the time you are born, you naturally become acquainted with your worth and have no fears about your future or how people view you. The concept of failure doesn't exist. When my daughter was learning to walk, she would try and fall and then try again and fall again until she succeeded. She didn't think approval was necessary, although she enjoyed my praise of her effort. She just set her intention of accomplishing her goal and worked toward it every day.

While I can't say I gave her self-esteem, I can say that the praise I gave her definitely improved her self-esteem, which means that I provided her support and added to her confidence. When we grow older, we have to remove limited ways of thinking that are taught through our fears. Self-esteem allows children to attempt new things without fear of failing or rejection and it gives them a starting point to manage troubles they may encounter on their life's journey.

All of this matters greatly since it determines what kind of person you will be in the future: people with high confidence believe they are worthy and see themselves as equal to others. They understand that they may be limited in some areas, but they expect to grow and improve without being entirely perfect. Those with low self-esteem generally experience self-disparagement, self-dissatisfaction, self-hatred, and self-rejection. They don't see themselves as equal and can be susceptible to drug and alcohol abuse, mental problems, suicide, and violence.

Healthy Self-Esteem

Having healthy self-esteem means that you see and love yourself as a worthy person. You become optimistic and surround yourself with others who appreciate you for who you are. You also get a good handle on your life and recognize that challenges are opportunities to grow.

If you think highly of yourself, you probably like the way you look, even if you don't fit the media's image of beauty. This strong outlook allows you to spend your time and energy discovering how to develop healthy relationships, gain appropriate independence from your parents, and challenge yourself physically and mentally. These things can be done without worrying about whether or not you look good to others. Developing these parts of yourself, setting goals, and working toward your goals can all help you boost your self-esteem.

An affirmative, confident attitude also helps breed strong self-esteem. Instead of feeling like a loser because you made a mistake, know that a mistake is a single event and not a way of life for you. Instead of viewing certain events as failures, see them as opportunities to grow and mature. While we all wrestle with self-doubt from time to time, we must aim to feel good about ourselves most of the time. India Arie has three songs that I love: "Video," "I Am Not My Hair," and "Private Party." I listen to these songs when I am feeling less than confident and I always emerge anew. Being aware of what brings you joy and keeps you healthy, alongside searching for the best ways to accomplish your dreams, is a great combination for building self-esteem.

Low Self-Esteem

Wishing you were someone else, wanting to change how you look, thinking you aren't smart enough or even that you aren't good enough to be part of the "cool" crowd: these are just a few examples of negative or low self-esteem. I call this a thinking disorder that causes an individual to think that he or she is inadequate, unlovable, and incompetent. If not properly corrected right away, these negative views will saturate your every thought, producing defective assumptions and ongoing self-defeating behavior.

Low Self-Esteem Triggers

What influences a person's self-esteem to change as they get older? For small children, it's their families and school. Family life influences your ability to communicate, sets your expectations for praise and discipline, and impacts how you think of yourself. Research has shown that families who aren't affectionate with one another tend to produce children who either seek attention or avoid it at all costs. Reversely, families that eat dinner together and have conversations are more likely to produce children who are comfortable expressing themselves.

For teenagers, puberty and development are major influences on their self-esteem. Many teenagers struggle with body image and their development. The changes they undergo, coupled with the desire to feel accepted and loved, can tempt anyone to compare oneself to others. The problem with this is that not everybody develops at the same time or in the same way, so standards cannot be the same either.

Still, others' expectations can sway our self-image, because our parents, family, and teachers might be too focused on what they want from us. Your parents may want you to look a certain way or make a certain weight for a sports team. Family members who struggle with their own body image often criticize their kids looks by making statements like, "Why do you keep your hair in your face?" or "You shouldn't wear your pants like that." Teachers often crush the spirits of teens with comments like, "How could you be so stupid?" These can all influence a person's self-esteem, especially if they don't feel validated by their families. Add in negative comments and hurtful teasing from their classmates and peers, and you have the perfect formula for low self-esteem. These hurtful comments often come from the source's own feelings of inadequacy, but they don't realize how much they can affect another individual's body image and self-esteem.

Body Image

Do you look at yourself in the mirror and say, "I am perfect just the way I am?" Or do you say, "I wish I were more toned, but overall I like the way I look?" It is healthy to look at your imperfections and want to improve them. What is unhealthy is when you see your imperfections and feel like you must hide or you can't be seen in public. We often put ourselves down, because we compare ourselves to others, and sometimes, it's easier to criticize your looks instead of embracing them. But when you get stuck on the negative, you'll get in the habit of bringing yourself down. Always remember that self-esteem greatly affects your mental health and how you behave.

Body image is how you view your physical self, including whether or not you believe you are attractive or others like your looks. It is closely linked to self-esteem since some people think they need to change how they look to feel good about themselves. The reality is that they need to change the way they see their bodies and how they think about themselves.

Let's talk about a few ways to do this:
1. *Understand that your body was created differently on purpose*: While we are supposed to have the same number of eyes, ears, and limbs, we don't have the same size portions. One person's breasts are bigger while another person's legs may be longer.

2. *Shift your focus*: Your body is uniquely yours, no matter what shape or size it comes in. Focus on the strength, health, and uniqueness of your body. When I look at my own hands, I know I have big knuckles and I don't really like them, but I also see that I have really nice nail beds that I never polish, because I love to see the free edge that I have. I can't change my hands, so I focus on what I love about them.
3. *Set goals to implement changes in things you are not happy with*: If you want to get fit or shed some pounds, make a plan to exercise five days a week and eat healthy. Sounds simple, right? If you make a realistic and reasonable goal like losing two pounds per week, you can reach a healthy weight in no time. Plus, you can keep track of your progress!
4. If you *can't change them, embrace them*: We are all unique and original—that's one of the best parts about being human. We certainly don't have to show all of our flaws to the world, but we can embrace them by continuing to be who we are and who we want to be. Tyra Banks was destined to be a supermodel, but guess what? She has cellulite. Her book, *Tyra's Beauty Inside and Out,* changed my life as a teenager, because she was so transparent. She showed her face up close without any makeup and talked about never going down the catwalk without something to cover her cellulite in the back. Still, she embraced her flaws and made the decision to pursue her goals anyway. Magazines simply airbrushed her cellulite away and she enjoyed a great career as a supermodel.

How to Improve Your Self-Esteem

You must be proactive in order to improve your self-esteem. You are the only one who can stop the negative comments coming from within. Remind yourself that you are more than what you look like or what you have or haven't done.

Building self-esteem can be done over time. Start by giving yourself three compliments a day. At a size sixteen, I still tell myself I love my curves. I turn from side-to-side and admire them every morning. I remind myself that my smile is the best smile in the world and that no one in the world has a bigger heart than I do. If you have a disability, focus on your senses, your intelligence, and other parts of your body that aren't affected; in fact, embrace your disability! We all have reasons to celebrate.

Finally, consider the consequences of your wrong decisions: drinking and doing drugs while operating a vehicle can lead to serious injury or death. Sex may lead to pregnancy, STD's, or HIV. Joining gangs leads to bad behavior and illegal activity, even jail. Dropping out of school removes your best chance to be a successful person later in life.

Think for yourself; it's worth it. Sticking to your values is not always going to be easy, but you will be happier if you do. Only you know what is best for you so value and respect yourself to avoid making bad decisions that may affect the rest of your life.

Where Can I Get Help?

Sometimes, low self-esteem becomes too much to handle alone. You may feel depressed and become anti-social. You may have unhealthy eating habits or negative body image. You may even indulge in alcohol and drugs to escape feelings of worthlessness. If you're feeling this way, asking for help is not a sign of weakness. Go to your parents, a favorite teacher, counselor, religious leader, mentor, coach, guidance therapist, or friend—anyone who doesn't judge you and listens to you. These people can provide positive feedback about your body, skills, and abilities. Let them assist your mind and emotions while you put your self-image into perspective.

If you need someone right away but don't have anyone you trust, call a teen crisis hotline. A quick Google search or dialing 211 from your phone can provide you options for both local and national hotlines. The most important thing is to get yourself the help you need.

Moving Forward

I asked a group of adults what would have helped develop their self-esteem as teenagers. Here are some of their answers:

- Being reassured that I mattered.

- More encouragement.

- Direct, open, and honest conversations with my parents.

- Playing sports.

- Having engaged, non-judgmental parents.

- Being told that I am valued.

- Friends or someone willing to say, "Hey, I'm an ugly duckling too."

- Having parents to invest time, love, and wisdom.

- Affirming and nurturing comments from both parents about my intellectual prowess, beauty, and positive spirit.

- Parents being interested in what I was doing and feeling (my cares, concerns, and questions) instead of assuming that I was a bright and resilient child who would figure stuff out on my own.

- Patience from others.

As you can see, messages about our self-esteem from our teen years leave lasting impressions into our adult years. You are not alone in your struggle to love yourself. Remember that self-esteem is important for everyone—keep working on building yours.

REVIEW QUESTIONS AND ASSESSMENT

Chapter Five
Self Esteem: Ladies Love Themselves First

1. What is self-esteem? _____
_____

2. True or False:
   Being disappointed in yourself is proof you have low self-esteem.
   _____

3. What is high self-esteem?
   _____
   _____
   _____
   _____

4. What is low self-esteem?
   _____
   _____
   _____
   _____

5. What are two characteristics of people with healthy self esteem?

   _____   _____

Let's assess your positive self-esteem.
Ask yourself these questions:

1. Do I believe in my morals and values?
2. Am I able to act in my best interest?
3. Do I genuinely enjoy my own company?
4. Do I participate in a mixture of activities and events?
5. Do I feel equal to others as a person?
6. Am I able to resist peer-pressure and negativity from others?
7. Do I believe in my ability to handle challenges?
8. Am I perceptive of the needs of others?
9. Am I able to adapt and be flexible in changing situations?
10. Am I happy, active, and passionate?
11. Do I enjoy life?
12. Am I overly sensitive to criticism?
13. Am I afraid to make a mistake?
14. Am I overly critical of others?
15. Do I blame others for everything?
16. Do I often feel persecuted?
17. Do I fear competition or trying new things?
18. Do I seek out praise?
19. Am I timid or withdrawn?
20. Do I need approval to be myself?
21. Am I jealous or possessive?
22. Do I have difficulty maintaining friendships and loving relationships?

Answering these questions honestly will help you assess your self-esteem and let you know if you are in need of some internal reexamination.

Notes

CHAPTER SIX

Social Media: Ladies Use the Internet Responsibly

We all love social media: it's fun, easy to use, and a great way to keep in touch and promote businesses. Add in the free factor and it's golden. However, social media can also be hurtful, dangerous, and deadly. While we say, "It's just entertainment" or "I use it casually," there are millions of people who misuse social media. From participating in online challenges to sharing videos, text messages, and photos, our interactions on social media often give us false senses of security that make us over-share information about what we are doing and where we are. There should always be rules, regulations, and common sense governing how we use the Internet.

Challenges on Social Media

Let's talk about some of the social media challenges that have been going around:

1. ***The Pretty Face Challenge:*** this is the challenge where people take a collage of pictures of themselves and post it on social media. You would think this challenge would be fun and light-hearted, and it is for the most part, until

some bully makes this comment: "Some people think they are pretty, and they are not." A passing thought that is mean and unnecessary and can really mess up someone's day.

2. ***The Cinnamon Challenge:*** I will admit I tried this one, because I love cinnamon, but I had no idea of the pain that I was in for. I had never taken a teaspoon of cinnamon before, and it was so painful I thought I was going to die. Why did I do it? Because I was challenged and I thought it would be harmless. Of course, I didn't die, but there were several people who ended up in the hospital because of that seemingly harmless challenge.

3. ***The Ice Bucket Challenge:*** this challenge went viral and flooded my timeline on all social media forms. I thought it was for a wonderful cause. Then I saw a news report about a young man with autism who was bullied into taking the challenge, but instead of ice and water, the liquid in the bucket was soda and urine. There are also videos of huge buckets falling on people by mistake and seriously injuring them. These videos have millions of views and shares, allowing people to instantly see the humiliation and then continue to spread it.

4. ***The Fire Challenge:*** I never quite understood how setting yourself on fire was entertainment, but the videos went viral and landed parents in jail for either neglect or child endangerment. People were severely burned and did irreparable damage to themselves—another example of how following a trend can be deadly.

Bullying on Social Media

Bullying on social media has been in the national spotlight since several high profile teen bullying stories made the news. The sad reality is that social media is open to bad people and good people alike, and when we add in the 24/7 access from our Internet-connected devices, we may have a recipe for disaster.

Two cases from the last few years have stood out to me. In one, a young girl in Florida jumped from a cement factory tower to her death because she was being bullied. The bullying was so bad that she thought death was the only way out. Reports claimed she was terrorized relentlessly for months by as many as fifteen girls, both physically and online. Her mother closed her Facebook account and moved her to another school, but since social media isn't limited to where we are physically, the cyber bullying continued.

Another case involved a special needs girl in Texas, who was bullied mercilessly by her classmates via text message. She had overcome many medical obstacles and participated in sports and cheerleading; yet, instead of being inspired by her, her classmates started bullying her. In both cases, the parents of the bullied girls took measures to stop the torture, and yet the bullying continued. Why? Because the Internet made it easy for them.

Bullying is unacceptable and punishable by jail time and fines for teens, as well as their parents or guardians.

Sex on Social Media

One thing we must realize is that everything we put on the Internet and social media is for the world to see. I don't care how many blocks you have on your settings. Once you have texted, e-mailed, or shared something, it can be viewed by the person who receives it and whomever they show it to, not to mention the people who have remote access to your phone at the phone company. Nothing is private!

Years ago, I lost my phone and wanted the pictures of my grandmother that I had stored on it before she had passed away.

I called my phone company and they were able to send me the photos along with those I thought I had deleted. In recent and more horrible news, several celebrities' phones were hacked, and their nude photos were released to the world. These were pictures that were stored privately on their phone and linked to an Internet source that was supposed to be safe. The creators of the phone can't even tell us how this is possible.

Everything that we put on the Internet is stored somewhere. Deleting it from your phone does not delete it from the Internet. Every now and then, we hear about public officials who have lied about affairs never happening or claiming it was one-time affair, only to have someone hack into their accounts and pull up emails or messages that show a pattern lasting five years or more.

With that being said, too often, I see people sharing videos with sexual content. Very few know the actual ages of the people in the videos and that makes everyone who shares it susceptible to an investigation from the Internet Crimes Against Children Division of their local police department. When we share sexual content of anyone under eighteen years old, we are sharing child pornography and are held responsible for that. This includes texting photos of breast and vaginal areas. You are also accountable for reporting photos sent to you that are sexual in nature. Your boyfriend sending you a photo of his penis is against the law. Saying "I didn't know" is not a defense.

Sex Trafficking on Social Media

Believe it or not, social media is a new forum for sex trafficking. Predators watch teens very closely: they know what you are wearing, they know when you have had an argument with your parents, they know your financial struggles as well as a host of other things, *because* these are things you post on your social media pages. Predators are more in tune with you than you realize.

Every time I hear of a teen girl being kidnapped, my heart drops. These young women are often stolen and forced into sex trafficking by someone who has lured them into a false sense of trust based on Internet profiles. You accept him because he is cute and says all the right things in his messages to you. Or, he sets up a fake profile using the photo of a young, pretty girl, who asks you if you want to make money. Sometimes, the predator will ask you to make "adult videos." Once you start to engage with "her," she introduces you to her "boyfriend," but the guy you meet may very likely be a pimp.

Once you meet this guy, it is literally too late to save yourself. He will give you money, nice clothes, even a place to live. What he doesn't tell you is that those are not gifts, they are purchases and he will decide how you repay it. Unfortunately, for many young girls, that means being drugged and sold into sex trafficking.

Things to Remember

Here are a few rules to govern yourself by:

1. *Don't share passwords*: I don't care if the person is your best friend. They're your best friend today, but you don't know what tomorrow will bring.
2. *Don't spread it even if it's true*: Rumors hurt, and no matter how accurate the information is, you don't know the entire story. Spreading someone's business on social media is harmful and hurtful.
3. *Don't engage with mean people*: Some people have an unhealthy relationship with social media and take it very seriously and personally because it is all they have. Engaging with them can result in fights and unnecessary drama.
4. *Don't accept friend requests from people who you don't personally know*: People create fake profiles just to get to know

your business. They may plot against you and use your information to harm you later.

5. *Be aware of people who are full of compliments*: A complete stranger who compliments you in a private message may sound wonderful and boost your ego, but the reality is, they want something and you may not want to give that something.
6. *Don't post things you don't want people who are not your friends to see*: It is very easy to screenshot or copy and paste your post.
7. *Make sure to use and update your security choices*: You are responsible for what's posted on your page and what you allow yourself to be tagged in.
8. *Nothing is private*: When you send a text message to your significant other, it can be viewed by someone at the phone company who looks through your account. Think about the many examples of our political officials.
9. *Never meet with anyone you have met online without your parents or guardians*: You don't know who is really on the other end of that computer. They may be posting pictures of their daughter and her adventures. They may be posting pictures of their nephew and his adventures. But you may get to the meeting spot and find yourself face-to-face with a forty-seven-year-old man who means only to harm you.

Bottom Line

These networking sites can provide you with sociability and a platform for self-expression. Within minutes, you can create profiles and upload your thoughts, videos, and photos. You can make contact with current friends, old friends, and also new friends you meet online. With all of your technological skills, you may think you are ready to face the world; in fact, your online skills are most likely better than your parents', so you probably aren't open about your online activities.

You may not have the people skills or general wisdom to conduct yourself sensibly on such a public forum—while you may know more about computers, you do not know more about life. This leaves you vulnerable to the attacks of cyber bullies and online predators, because, just like in real life, you cannot anticipate what may come of your online posts. You can't always comprehend what information is private versus public or that you are unknowingly creating virtual leashes for yourself by checking in everywhere you go.

Responsible online behaviors and practices require maturity and communication. You must remember that everything you put on your social media sites can also be viewed by your school and employer. They are responsible for weeding out people who won't be a good fit for their organizations and your social sites may give them all the reasons they need to leave you out of the fold. I have denied several applicants for employment because I discovered through their social sites that they are underage drinkers who use too much profanity, do drugs, "turn-up" too much, and have no respect for authority. Once again, keep in mind that, once you put it out there, it is there forever and it certainly isn't deleted just because you pressed "Delete." You can't even delete your Facebook account—you can only deactivate it. When you return, your content returns.

Social media brings out the best and worse in people. While you may make great connections, the threat of predators (pedophiles, sociopaths, murders, etc.) is real. Never meet up with someone you have met online. There are too many stories of young women being killed, sold into sex trafficking, and raped, all because they trusted someone they met on social media.

REVIEW QUESTIONS

Chapter Six
Social Media: Ladies Use The Internet Responsibly

1. How are social media challenges harmful?

   _____

   _____

2. Why is it important not to share sexual videos, no matter how harmless you think they are?

   _____

   _____

3. Fill in the blanks.

   Bullying is _____ and _____ with _____ and _____ for teens and their parents

4. True or False:
   My text messages are safe because I have a lock on my phone.

5. True or False:
   Once I delete it, it is gone forever.

6. Who investigates videos shared on the internet that appear to have minors naked or being sexual in them?
   _____

7. Why do you have to report receiving explicit photos of anyone under eighteen? _____
   _____

8. Name two ways to govern yourself on social media.

   1. _____
   2. _____

Notes

Professional Development: Ladies Are Prepared for What They Want

I once contracted with a company who asked me to train their youth participants in professional development for job hunting. My goal was to teach them how to get a job and keep it. Let me say this: one of the most impactful things you can do as you hunt for jobs is to make sure that you are neat and organized, both mentally and physically. Visual presentation is key. Your applications and resumes are oftentimes the only items your potential employer has to understand who you are.

Applications

If you are mailing in your applications or taking them in, they should not be wrinkled, and they should never be folded or dog-eared on the corners. All of this makes a difference. When you are being hired, people want to know that you are presenting your best self and a stained application does not present that. Also, make sure you have filled the application out completely, leaving no blank spaces, and double check for spelling mistakes and wrong phone numbers.

Resumes

Your resumes are an extension of your application. Make sure your spelling and grammar are correct. Knowing the difference between "they are," "they're," "there," and "their" can really make a difference on whether or not you get a job.

Once you have created your resume, save it under your first and last name. This way, a potential employer can easily find your files when searching on their computers.

E-mail

Often times, your first contact with a potential employer will be through an email. Make sure you have a good email address that cannot be misinterpreted or offensive. Your first name and last name @ a credible e-mail subscription is best. So, janedoe@gmail.com is much better than ilovehorses@gmail.com or Sexxxylady@gmail.com. Now, your email may tell your employer that you do love horses or you believe you are sexy, but that's not what they're looking for when they're trying to search for your name and application to contact you for an interview.

You also want to be sure that your email doesn't have any profanity or insinuate anything inappropriate or irrelevant. For instance, if you have triple X's in your email address, that can send a message that you don't necessarily want to convey.

Phone Numbers

Your phone number should be on your application and the resume, and it should be a direct number to your voicemail. Do not provide the number to your grandmother's house unless you live there. If you must give this number, prepare your grandmother to answer the call with pen and paper at the ready, and remind her or whoever else that may answer the phone to keep their television sets down or on mute when answering; a potential employer will be thrown off by background noises or someone who takes five minutes to grab a pen and piece of paper.

It's always easy to set up a Google number that goes directly to your cell phone in the event you need to use it. Keep the purpose of this voicemail in mind. While we all enjoy hearing a good song, there should never be a situation where an employer calls your phone and they hear inappropriate music. They also should not have to listen to three minutes of that to get to the beep.

Keep your voicemail simple: "Hi, you have reached the voicemail of [insert name]. Please leave a message at the tone with your name, number and a brief detailed message." That's it. It should never have details of where you are nor should it say anything like, "If this is Bobby, don't call me again." A potential employer will look at this as being childish and they will not hire you.

Dress Code

In person, your outward appearance makes a huge difference in whether or not you get a job. Be sure to dress professionally. Pay attention to your hair: make sure it is combed neatly. If you're going to wear braids, make sure they are fresh and pulled out of your face. No do-rags or scarves. Your hair should be a natural color; no blue or pink hair or exaggerated extensions.

Close-toed shoes are mandatory. Do not wear platform shoes. Whatever you choose should be flat or have no more than a three-inch heel, and they must also be clean. In addition, make sure your clothing is not tight or low-cut. Business attire only, meaning slacks, an appropriately-length skirt, or dress that comes to your knees. Shirts should have collars and should not be sweater material. No pajamas or jeans.

Hands Free

Be conscious of what you're holding when you walk into an interview. Us ladies, often have our purses or briefcases, some type of beverage, our resumes, or perhaps even our keys still in our hands when we walk into an interview. This is unacceptable.

Simply take in a folder with your resume or application, your car key that opens the door to your car, your ID, social security card, and any references. Tuck everything inside the folder so you have one central place for it all and can hand them to your interviewer. If you only take the key that opens your car door, it won't be bulky. That is all you need to take inside. Leave your briefcase unless they have asked you to bring additional papers or books. Finish your beverage in the car and leave your cup in there. You do not want to walk into an interview with your hands so full that you cannot shake hands with the person in front of you.

Social Media

When you are applying for a job, you must clean up your social media. Photos that depict you drinking, smoking, and holding up obscenities (middle finger) must be removed, alongside any footage or record of fights, racist rants, religion bashings, profanity, or gossip about your child(ren)s' other parent.

Your social media is a representation of your personality. Potential employers and schools use it to get an insight into the person they are bringing into their organization. Before you post, ask yourself, "Is this something I want my dream job or school to see?"

Quitting Your Old Job

You will likely have multiple jobs as you search for what you want to do in life. When you decide that you want to leave your current place of employment, be sure to leave in a way that doesn't stop you from being hired by other companies.

The proper way to end your employment relationship with a company is to speak with your supervisor and let them know you are giving them your two weeks' notice, after which you will be leaving. Two weeks gives them enough time to post a new job announcement to fill your position and calculate any money they owe you from sick or vacation time due to you.

Most companies do not allow people who quit without notice to return to employment with them. Also, when potential employers call them regarding your past work history, they will discover that you left in poor standing and are less likely hire you.

Drugs

While there may be many medical marijuana clinics in your area and you may have a prescription from your doctor to consume it (if you are eighteen and over), still consider the consequences. Many companies have drug testing requirements and policies and will still deny you employment if you fail their drug test. Being able to legally consume marijuana does not obligate companies to employ you.

Applying For a Job

When looking for a job, there will be several things you will need to have in your possession:

1. *Application*: Make sure you fill it out completely. If there are questions you are unsure about, find the answers before you submit your application. If a section does not apply to you, write "N/A" so the employer knows you saw it and that it does not apply. Any blanks on the page can be mistaken as an incomplete application.

2. *Identification card*: The card must list your current address. Your employer will make a copy of it and all of the information should be current and correct.
3. *Social security card*: This will be requested and you will need it in order to be paid. Have it ready with your ID card so you don't have search around when it is time to produce it.
4. *Three personal and three non-related references*: Make sure you have their first and last names. Know their phone numbers, addresses, and job titles. Also, let your references know that you are listing them.

The Interview

Before your interview, take time to find out about the company you are applying for. Go to their website and read through it so you can answer questions about your qualifications according to what they are looking for. Know who the key people in the company are so you can say "Hello" to them if you see them in passing.

Once inside the interview, sit up straight with a notebook and pen in your hand. Take one or two-word notes to help you remember questions you want to ask at the end or things you want to mention when you state your qualifications. Answer questions with short and concise statements. The interviewer will ask you to elaborate if they want to know more. Do not speak negatively about your current or past employers and do not speak about your personal life.

After the interview, go straight to the post office and mail your interviewer a "Thank you" card. Mention one thing personal (something you learned or a funny thing the interviewer said), and then, thank him or her for making you feel comfortable and making time for you. Finally, let them know that you look forward to working with them in the near future.

Additional Documents
1. *School transcripts*: If the job posting requires your school transcripts, be sure to take them to the interview so that they can be copied. Always have the original on hand just in case they won't accept a copy.
2. *TB test results*: If your potential employer requires a tuberculosis test, they will let you know. Have the test done immediately, because you will have to go back to that doctor after a few days to have it read for your results. Every doctor's office is different and it may take a few additional days for you to get the written proof of the results.
3. *Background checks*: Some employers require clearance from the Department of Justice in order for you to work for them. They will not hire you until this is complete and comes back to them with your clearance, so do not delay this process. A local police station or sub-station on a college campus may be the most convenient place to have this done.

Final Thoughts

Job-hunting doesn't have to be difficult and being prepared is a great way to have a fair chance at the position you want. Be sure to smile, speak well, and show them you are the best candidate.

REVIEW QUESTIONS

Chapter Seven
Professional Development: Ladies
are Prepared for What They Want

1. Fill in the blanks:
Make sure you are _____ and _____, _____, and _____.

2. True or False:
Dog-eared corners on a resume are not presenting your best self.

3. Resumes should be saved under your _____ and _____ name.

4. What should your email address be for potential employers?
_____

5. Name a resource for an alternate phone number.
_____

6. What is "business attire?" Give examples:
_____   _____
_____

7. What does it mean to be "hands free" for an interview?
   _____

8. Name three things that should be in your interview folder:
   _____   _____

   _____

9. What does it mean to clean up your social media?
   _____

   _____

10. What is the first thing you should do when you leave an interview?
    _____

    _____

11. Name three additional documents:
    _____   _____

    _____

Notes

Goal Setting: Ladies Make Plans

Goal setting is one of the most important habits you can create for yourself as a young person transitioning into adulthood. It keeps you focused and constantly in the space of accomplishing your goals.

I recently heard Laila Ali—world boxing champion and daughter of one of the greatest fighters of all time, Muhammad Ali--speaking about the moment she decided to become a boxer. Laila had grown up on the good side of town, but she made the decision to live on her own and be self-sufficient. She set out to go to cosmetology school to get her license as a nail technician and hoped to eventually open up several salons or a spa.

At the time, she didn't have a car, so she purchased one for four hundred dollars. It was an old, beat-up car that didn't even run well enough to get it to the gas station once she purchased it. But, she did it anyway and figured out a way to get through at least a couple of months with this beat-up car.

Most people thought that she was destined to be a boxer because of her father, but that wasn't the case. In fact, it was when she attended a live boxing match featuring Mike Tyson and saw women fighters in the pre-fight that her interest was sparked. She was so excited watching them fight that it consumed her thoughts.

She decided she would secretly train, knowing that she had a lot to prove. People looked at her differently, since she was Muhammad Ali's daughter. She decided to leave school and pursue her boxing career, in which she eventually became a world champion boxer. She never wanted to be a boxer, but once she set her goal to be a world champion, she was determined to make it happen. She was clear on her end result, planned for it, and made moves that were only goal-focused. In fact, at every moment of her life, even when she was not pursuing boxing, Laila was focused and hard working.

Here's what we can learn from Laila Ali: the first step is to have your goal or goals in mind. Focus on no more than six major objectives, all of which should be things you can focus on and accomplish within a year. Be clear and specific. Here's an outline to get you started:

1. Mental Goals:
2. Physical Goals:
3. Spiritual Goals:
4. Emotional Goals:
5. Financial Goals:
6. Professional Goals:

Your goals should be broken down in such a way that you can see yourself accomplishing them within one year. Here's how to do that:

1. *Pinpoint what you want:* Be exact, no generalizations.
2. *Decide what you're willing to sacrifice:* When Laila decided to go to cosmetology school, she sacrificed her time and comfort, and she jumped on a bus. Eventually, she

sacrificed her money to get a car to make things a little easier for her.

3. *Set a date:* Decide when you want your goal to be accomplished by. Six months, one year—it doesn't matter. Set the date. Here's the thing: if you don't accomplish your goal by this time, you don't change the goal. You simply change the date.
4. *Make a plan for weekly, monthly, and quarterly increments:* You want to be able to check in at those points to be sure you're on track.
5. *Make daily affirmations:* Affirm what it is that you want. Say it over and over again to yourself throughout the day. Stick post-its in your car, in your locker, on your mirror, on your fridge, inside your textbooks, wherever you look so that you can stay focused.

How to Get Started

1. *Mental:* Your first goal must focus on mental wellness. One goal you might set is to have better conversations or to make better friends. The best way to grow mentally is to read and talk to people smarter than you. Who are you going to speak to? What are you going to learn from your mentors? Are you going to read more books? (If you are a teenaged, I definitely suggest that you read *Seven Habits of Highly Effective Teens* by Sean Covey.) When talking with your mentors, let them know that you have decided to become a better person with their help and you want to know what's in their library. Whatever the case may be, have very specific conversations with them.
2. *Spiritual:* Your spiritual goal may mean praying every day or meditating; it may mean reading Scriptures or other spiritual books that help you grow in your everyday life.

Whatever it is, figure out at least twelve texts that you can read for the year, whether its twelve books, twelve scripture chapters, or twelve books of the Bible. Whatever twelve you choose, plan to finish one within thirty days. Commit to growing into a more spiritually mature person.

3. *Physical*: Say you have a goal to lose one hundred pounds. In a year's time, this is only two pounds a week, which is really about walking thirty minutes a day and eating more fruits and vegetables, as stated in the previous chapter. The point is to set a goal and to check in with yourself in increments. That first month, make sure that your hard work has helped you lose eight pounds. When you set that quarterly goal, you want to be in between twenty to twenty-five pounds as you move towards your hundred-pound mark.

4. *Emotional*: Strive to be a better person emotionally than you were when you started the goal. Sometimes, that means taking time to center yourself so you're not flying off the handle, holding grudges, or getting angry with people for long periods of time. This goal is meant to get your emotional intelligence together.

5. *Financial*: Let's just say that you want to save twenty dollars out of each weekly or biweekly paycheck. At the end of the year, you should be able to save five hundred twenty dollars. Now, that may not sound like a lot, but that's still five hundred dollars more than you planned, and when you get consistent, you can always add more. Sometimes, you need to start small, and if you can do more than twenty, great! It's all about getting a strong start.

6. *Professional*: As young people, we tend to think about getting a job instead of doing something toward our career. I'm a firm believer that some component of what you want

to do in the future can be found right now. Say you want to serve as a talk show host: as a high school student, you could start a lunch break club that allows you to host guest panelists for thirty minutes. The reality is that most talk shows only last about forty-five minutes when you consider commercials. So, a thirty-minute lunch period is plenty of time to have people gather in quickly, open, have a discussion on a couple of topics with a guest (about fifteen to twenty minutes), and close. Bam! You've already got your start. In today's society, someone can even use their phone to record your show and put it on YouTube or they can even do a live broadcast on Periscope. It's very simple and easy to do.

Another great thing to boost your professionalism is to volunteer and participate in the areas you want to further yourself. Let's say you want to be a lawyer: colleges love activities on your resume and college application. Contact a lawyer and try to get an internship position in their practice on Saturdays or during the summers. These are great opportunities for you to further your career before you even start it.

Accountability

One of the best ways to ensure your goals are accomplished is to have an accountability partner. This is a person who helps you keep commitments to yourself. They don't accept your excuses and they push you to your max. Be sure to have this sort of motivator in your corner.

REVIEW QUESTIONS

Chapter Eight
Goal Setting: Ladies Make Plans

1. Name three things you learned from the story about Laila Ali:

    1. _____
    2. _____
    3. _____

2. What are the six areas of your goal list?

    _____   _____   _____

    _____   _____   _____

3. Name and describe the steps to accomplishing your goals:

    1. _____
    2. _____
    3. _____
    4. _____
    5. _____

4. What actions are you going to take to accomplish your goals based on the steps above?

    1. _____
    2. _____

3. _____
4. _____
5. _____
6. _____

7. Name a benefit to having an accountability partner.

_____

Notes

Bullying: Ladies Don't Intentionally Hurt People

Bullying is the act of being an argumentative and overbearing person who constantly harasses and induces fear in people who are not likely to fight back. I must admit that I was a bit of a bully growing up, because I had once been insecure. I didn't really want to fight anyone, but bullying was an offensive tactic that kept the other bullies off of me. It was easier for me to pick on people who I knew wouldn't fight back than to stand up to the real bullies.

Being Bullied

There are many ways to handle bullies. You can try to work it out, but bullies are not likely to change their behavior, so be sure to have a back-up plan that includes help from your parents or teachers. If you are being attacked at school, your teachers are your first line of defense. Find one you trust and let them know what is going on. Take a friend with you if it will make you more comfortable. If you are being bullied in your neighborhood, tell your parents or guardians. There is absolutely no shame in being bullied and asking for help is not a sign of weakness—it is the ultimate statement of strength. Take the steps to get help so it doesn't continue.

If you are being verbally bullied, the first thing to remember is not to engage the conversation. Bullies want you to react, and when you don't, they start to realize that they "look" like bullies to others. Eventually, they lose interest when they don't succeed in upsetting you. As simple as it sounds, walking away from a bully is a strong approach.

Sometimes, it isn't possible to avoid the bully. After all, the reason they are able to affect us is because they are in the places we frequent. So, whether it is on the bus, at school, in your neighborhood, or local entertainment places, you may have to confront your bully with fear in your heart. Remember that bullies look for people who won't fight back, so standing up to them is often the best way to get them to leave you alone.

If you find yourself trapped by the bully, unable to escape, and you haven't been able to make a plan with your parents or other trusted adults, you may have to fight. The fight may not be about winning or losing but rather about survival. You have the right to live, study, go to school, and chill in a comfortable and safe environment, free from harassment, violence, discrimination, and bullying. While I don't condone fighting, I am a believer that, *sometimes*, you have to punch the problem right in the nose. Again, I don't encourage this and I hope there are other options to be exhausted first.

Instead, try to be strong and assertive and let them know you are *willing* to stand your ground. Have a strategy ahead of time that works for *you* to prevent isolation, fear, sadness, or anger, and act appropriately in the moment of confrontation

Cyber Bullying
Cyber bullying is when people are attacked, harassed, made to feel uncomfortable, threatened, and tormented by others who are using the Internet, numerous applications, mobile devices, video game counsels, and other interactive digital technologies. This is becoming more common and can show itself in various ways:

- Fake profiles to get to you
- Negative comments about you that damage your reputation and character
- Threats to harm you
- Stalking

These things can be dangerous and may require the involvement of local police, but you can start by deleting and blocking them and not accepting friend requests from people you don't know.

REVIEW QUESTIONS

Chapter Nine
Bullying: Ladies Don't Intentionally Hurt People

1. What is bullying?

   _____

2. Who can you go to for help if you are being bullied at school? _____   _____

3. Who can you go to for help if you are being bullied at home or in your neighborhood? _____

   _____

Fill in the blanks:

4. Bullies want you to _____.

5. Bullies are looking for people who _____

   _____ _____.

6. What is cyber bullying?

   _____

7. Describe three ways cyber-bullying shows itself?

   1. _____
   2. _____
   3. _____

Fill in the blanks:

While I don't _____ fighting when it is

_____ and think it should only be

_____

when all other options have been _____, I do

believe _____ yourself is a necessary

_____ _____.

Notes

CHAPTER TEN

Dating: Ladies Know They Can't Turn a Cowboy into a Prince

You are now at an age when your feelings lead your actions and reactions more than any other time in your life. Your feelings may cloud your better judgment and present themselves as absolute truths. When dating, you have to remember that your emotions will lie to you: they don't know everything and many things will feel good, but won't be good *for* you.

Dating happens. Adults know it, and we want you to be smart about it. So, here are a few things that are rarely talked about when young ladies start dating.

Emotions

Boys are taught to hold in and hide their emotions. From the moment they can walk, they are told, "Big boys don't cry. Suck it up, shake it off, toughen up, stop crying"—they are told everything except, "Come here and tell me what's wrong."

Young men are taught to act, rather than feel. The only emotion they are encouraged to share is anger and they are rarely comforted when sad or hurt. So naturally, they may not know how to comfort you when you are sad or hurting, because they have never had any type of practice or examples in expressing themselves.

Mindset

As a lady, you must consider the long-term effects of dating. This begins with understanding the guy you are interested in. Here are some questions to ask about him:

1. Where was he raised?
2. What kind of community did he grow up in?
3. How has he been affected by his environment?
4. What kind of family was he born into and raised by?
5. Has he been trained to fight instead of cry?
6. Has he been trained to walk away to avoid losing?

My friend Rafer Owens once said, "Just because he has both parents doesn't mean he has a stable family. His father could've abused his mother. If he's been trained to walk away to avoid losing, then guess what? He will dump you to avoid losing an argument."

Anything that has gone on in his home could have affected him. All of this develops his mentality and are signs of who he is and how he's going to treat you. When you and your guy are having issues, examine his mentality. I know that this is a huge undertaking in high school, but remember that you can't make him into the person you want him to be. You can't love him hard enough. You can't make a cowboy a prince.

Real men want to work hard at school and work so they can be self-sufficient. High school boys are still trying to avoid gang violence, drugs, abuse, and becoming a statistic. If he wants to be a real man, he will focus on being unstoppable until gets an education, his own money, and his own transportation.

The truth is, your job as a lady is to be mission-minded as well and be set on the path to success. Handle your business, because you are an asset to men. Getting your hair and nails done may contribute to your beauty, but they don't make you an asset. Getting a college degree does. If you are already a teen mom, attending PTA meetings and making sure that your children are taken care of, makes you an asset.

Dating Violence

Domestic violence in teen dating is a huge problem, affecting youth in every community across the nation. One in four high school girls experience some form of physical, sexual, emotional, or verbal abuse while dating. Many of them are forced to deal with the after effects of being raped while on dates. Here are a few facts:

1. About 72% of eighth and ninth graders are "dating."
2. Young ladies between the ages of sixteen and twenty-four encounter the largest rate of intimate terrorism, almost triple the national average.
3. Violent behavior typically begins between the ages of twelve and eighteen.
4. The severity of intimate partner violence is often greater in cases where the pattern of abuse was established in adolescence.
5. Physically or sexually abused teen girls are six times more likely to become pregnant and twice as likely to get an STI.
6. Half of youth who have been victims of both dating violence and rape attempt suicide, compared to 12.5% of non-abused girls and 5.4% of non-abused boys.
7. Young victims of dating abuse often cannot apply for restraining orders.
8. Currently, only one juvenile domestic violence court in the country focuses exclusively on teen dating violence.

9. 66% of teens who have been in a violent relationship never told anyone about the abuse.
10. 81% of parents don't believe teen-dating violence is an issue.

While dating feels very "grown up," it can bring about adult situations that you aren't ready to deal with. Be sure to identify a woman you trust; you should be able to go to her at any moment's notice to talk things through and she will help you out of a bad situation.

Tips

Here are a few guidelines to help you stay out of trouble while dating:

1. *Turn down the intensity:* Kissing doesn't need to involve your tongues or leave your face area.

2. *Keep your boyfriend out of your bedroom:* Limit him to the common areas of your home, such as the living room and den.

3. *Choose group dating:* This helps you and your friends be accountable to one another. Keep each other in sight at all times and remind yourself not to do anything in secret that you wouldn't want to be public.

4. *If you are allowed to have your boyfriend in your room, keep your door open.*

5. *Be honest:* We lie to our parents to avoid trouble and uncomfortable conversations, as well as to keep the nice image that they have of us. Still, tell the truth about where you are going, who you are with, and what you are doing.

6. *Ask questions:* If your parents have a rule you don't like, don't whine, complain, or have an attitude. Those things show them that you are still not at a level of maturity they can trust. Instead, ask them to explain to you what their expectations are and how you can get a "Yes" the next time. The more you ask, the less likely you will be in trouble for something you weren't clear on.

7. *Value yourself:* When you cherish yourself, you won't need to find your value in other people and you will be less likely to compromise your beliefs and standards.

REVIEW QUESTIONS

Chapter Ten
Dating: A Lady Knows She Can't Turn a Cowboy into a Prince

1. Fill in the blank:
   When dating, you have to remember that your _____ lie to you.

2. What are three questions you should ask about someone you are dating?
   1. _____
   2. _____
   3. _____

3. Identify a few guidelines to help you have fun while dating:
   1. _____
   2. _____
   3. _____
   4. _____

4. Give five facts about dating violence:
   1. _____
   2. _____
   3. _____
   4. _____
   3. _____

Notes

Etiquette: Ladies Are Mindful

All ladies should know about etiquette. Author Amy Vanderbilt wrote the *Complete Book of Etiquette,* a great resource for proper etiquette in various situations. I highly recommend it, but for this chapter, we will just cover a few basics:

Introductions / Greetings
When meeting someone for the first time, it is important to leave a lasting, positive impression. As a lady, how you greet someone can define your relationship. A strong handshake says more than "Hello, nice to meet you." It shows the person that you are confident, polite, and caring.

Four Keys to a Great Introduction or Greeting
1. *Smile*: Smiles are welcoming and invite conversations to start
2. *Eyes contact*: This is a sign of respect to the person and shows that you are interested in what they are saying.
3. *A firm handshake*: This says you are confident and can handle yourself. A weak handshake says you don't want to be touched or you are not interested in further conversation.

If you are more familiar with the person and it is a casual environment, you can offer a hug instead of a handshake, when appropriate.

4. *Introduce yourself*: "Hello, my name is _____. How are you?" then *wait* for the answer. Waiting is key because many ask that question out of formality, but don't really care. When you wait for the answer, you make an instant connection with people.

Calling the Home of Your Friends and Their Parents

Most of your friends probably have their own cell phones and you call them in a relaxed and informal tone of voice. However, when you are calling their home phone number and they live with their parents or relatives, your tone and speech must be respectful. Here are a few tips:

1. Greet them by saying, "Hello Mr. or Mrs. Smith." If you don't know their last name, simply say, "Hello Ma'am or Sir."
2. Introduce yourself with your first and last name: "This is Jasmine Shaw."
3. Ask for the person you would like to speak to: "May I speak to Taylor, please?"
4. Once they respond, remember to say, "Thank you."

Table Etiquette

Enjoying dinner at home or in public can be one of the most relaxing moments of your day. But these moments are, in a way, choreographed by common sense and good etiquette. Remember that your behavior affects the dining experience of everyone around you. Here are a few tips to practice at home that can easily become second nature everywhere you dine.

1. *Be on time*: Many places will not seat your party if everyone is not there, so your tardiness can delay dinner. It is also a sign that you don't value the time of the people you are with.
2. *Sit up straight*: No slouching!
3. *Elbows off the table*: Generally, you rest your hands in your lap during dinner conversations. If your elbows find their way onto the dining table, don't panic. Simply remove them.
4. *Put your napkin on your lap as soon as you are seated*: In some restaurants, the host or waiter will do this for you.
5. *Drink to your right and bread to your left*: It is possible that most people you are with won't know this. However, you can set the flow and others will follow.
6. *Close your mouth while chewing*: This sounds simple enough, but we often talk while eating and forget that people can see into our mouths.
7. *Let your date order for you*: In a world full of independent women, this isn't very popular. But think of it like this: as part of the conversation, you should be letting him know what you want to eat and he should be listening for the purpose of repeating your order back to your waiter.
8. *Speak in low tones*: Only your table should be able to hear your conversations.
9. *Silence your phone and put it away*: It is rude to spend time on your phone while having dinner. If you are expecting a call, let your dinner party know, put it on vibrate, and set it in your lap. You will be able to feel the vibrations.

Voice Projection

Often, we come from environments where we aren't heard as individuals, either because no one is listening or because we are drowned out by family, friends, or media devices. As a result, we tend to either speak too softly or too loudly. When we do get loud, we must consider where we are and who we are impacting.

When walking into a business, your voice should soften and decrease in volume. Business is being conducted and speaking loudly is disruptive. If you must be on your phone, the conversation should not be so personal that you would be embarrassed if someone overheard it.

Attitude

Believe it or not, attitude is directly related to success in life and business. Your attitude is really just an outward expression of your inward thoughts and beliefs. When you have a positive attitude, you self manage more effortlessly with the day-to-day ups and downs, and you bring cheerfulness into yourself. Positivity will also make it easier to steer clear of doubts and pessimistic thinking. In addition, people will *want* to be around you, because you are pleasant and contribute to a great environment.

REVIEW QUESTIONS

Chapter Eleven
Etiquette: Ladies are Mindful

Fill in the blank:
1. When meeting someone for the _____ time, it is important to leave a _____, _____ impression.

2. A handshake tells a person if you are _____, _____, and _____.

3. Name two keys to a great introduction or greeting:
   1. _____
   2. _____

4. Name the four steps to follow when calling your friends' homes:
   1. _____
   2. _____
   3. _____
   4. _____

5. Name three tips you can practice at home for table etiquette:
   1. _____
   2. _____
   3. _____

6. Fill in the blanks:
    When walking into a business, your voice should
    _____ and _____ in
    _____.

    Your attitude is really just an _____
    _____ of your inward _____ and
    _____.

Notes

Afterword

As a mom of boys, I think about the type of young ladies my sons will bring home. Will I like them? Will they remind me of me? Will they be goal-oriented and supportive? Or will they be the total opposite? As I assist my sons in becoming respectful gentlemen, it is important to me that they seek respectable young ladies with value *and* values: women with goals, proper etiquette, good hygiene, and high self-esteem. Still, I can't choose for my young men, so I make every effort to be a good woman every day and pray that I have set a standard for the women they will meet. Although *I Choose to be a Lady* was created for girls, it also holds great value for boys for this reason, whether they have good moms or not. This book lets them know the very minimum they should expect a woman to know.

I know firsthand that professional success is directly related to personal development. As a coach and mentor, I see a need for basic knowledge in adult women who don't have access to the kind of guidance and training that many take for granted. This foundational book is a gold mine that gives all young ladies a fighting chance to get approval from moms like me who expect the best *from* and *for* our sons. I look forward to reading the next one!

Nikki Woods
Senior Producer, Tom Joyner Morning
Show Nikki Woods Media

About the Author

Kiana Shaw is a three-time bestselling author, public speaker, master personal development coach, prevention and early intervention specialist, and mother. As a survivor of sexual abuse who once struggled with her own choices and self-esteem, Shaw now utilizes the experiences of her past to empower others who seek to elevate themselves in all aspects of their lives. Alongside being a coach and a mentor, she also provides women and girls throughout Southern California with tools for leadership and empowerment as the CEO of Village of Truth, Inc.

Shaw currently resides in Los Angeles with her daughter, Kayla Renee. She is an advocate of intentional parenting and strong family communication, and in 2015, she received the Wealthy Sisters Network's Parent Coach of the Year Award for her effective work in bringing harmony, love, and supportive dialogue back into struggling homes.

Author Connection

Kiana Shaw
CEO of LeadHERship Academy

PO Box 3615
Gardena, CA 90247
424-242-8879

Meet me online at:
www.KianaShaw.com
www.IChooseToBeALady.com
www.LeadHERshipAcademy.org

Check my websites for FREE downloads.

Be sure to join the LeadHERship Academy online to take the extensive course and receive your Certificate of Completion.

WE WANT TO HEAR FROM YOU!!!

If this book has made a difference in your life Kiana would be delighted to hear about it.

Leave a review on Amazon.com!

BOOK KIANA TO SPEAK AT YOUR NEXT EVENT!
Send an email to: booking@publishyourgift.com
Learn more about Kiana at:
www.KianaShaw.com

FOLLOW KIANA ON SOCIAL MEDIA

f TheKianaShawShow   CoachKianaShaw

"EMPOWERING YOU TO IMPACT GENERATIONS"
WWW.PUBLISHYOURGIFT.COM

www.ingramcontent.com/pod-product-compliance
Lightning Source LLC
Chambersburg PA
CBHW071520080526
44588CB00011B/1500